Managing Stress for Teens

Miriam Kinai

Copyright © 2009 Dr Miriam Kinai

All rights reserved.

All rights reserved under International Copyright Law. No part of this publication may be reproduced, stored in a retrieval system, transmitted in any way by any means – electronic, mechanical, photocopy, recording or otherwise – without prior written permission from the publisher except for brief quotations in critical reviews or articles.

All scripture is taken from the New King James Version. Copyright 1979, 1989, 1982 by Thomas Nelson, Inc. Used by permission. All rights reserved.

ISBN: 1477560858
ISBN-13: 978-1477560853

DEDICATION

Blessed be the God and Father

of our Lord Jesus Christ,

the Father of mercies

and God of all comfort,

who comforts us in all our tribulation,

that we may be able to comfort

those who are in any trouble,

with the comfort with which

we ourselves are comforted by God.

(2 Corinthians 1:3-4)

CONTENTS

Abbreviations   i

1. **ADDICTIVE SUBSTANCES**   Pg #1
   Alcohol
   Cigarettes
   Drugs
   Resisting Temptation
   Overcoming Addiction

2. **FAMILY**   Pg #22
   Family Background
   Being an Orphan
   Brothers & Sisters
   Excessive Responsibilities
   Abuse

3. **FEELINGS & EMOTIONS**   Pg #36
   Anger
   Anxiety & Worry
   Confusion
   Fear
   Feeling Inadequate
   Feeling like Giving Up
   Feeling Unloved
   Guilt
   Loneliness
   Love & Lust
   Low Self Confidence
   Revenge
   Sadness
   Shyness

4 **FRIENDS**   Pg #74
Negative Peer Pressure
Positive Peer Pressure
True & False Friends
High Expectations from Friends
How to Relax with Friends
Opposite sex relationships
Broken relationships

5 **LIFE & DEATH**   Pg #94
Abortion
Suicide
Death
Death of a Loved One
Sickness & Disability

6 **MONEY**   Pg #108
Not Having Money
Lack of School Fees

7 **PARENTS**   Pg #121
Obeying Parents
Pressure from Parents
Parents not Trusting You
Parents not Understanding You
Parents Fighting

8 **RELIGION**   Pg #135
The Lord God Almighty
Jesus Christ God's Son
The Holy Spirit
Feeling You Lack Faith
Living Right

9 **SCHOOL**   Pg #149
Bullying
Prefects

Obeying Teachers
Teachers Abusing Students
Preparing for Exams
Poor Academic Performance

10 SEX   Pg #165
Fighting Temptation
Fornication
Masturbation
Pornography
Homosexuality & Lesbianism
Sugar Daddies & Sweet Mommies
Stopping Sexual Sin
Teenage Pregnancy
Rape

11 SOCIETY   Pg #205
Celebrities
Fashion
Crime
Corruption
Cultural Practices
Global Warming & Pollution

12 YOU   Pg #226
Puberty
Body Shape & Self Image
Comparison Syndrome
Who am I?
Gender Realization
Why am I here?
Negative Thoughts & Words
Your Past
Your Future

ABBREVIATIONS

Genesis **Gen**

Exodus **Ex**

Leviticus **Lev**

Numbers **Num**

Deuteronomy **Deut**

Joshua **Josh**

Judges **Judg**

Ruth Ruth

1 Samuel **1 Sam**

2 Samuel **2 Sam**

1 Kings **1 Kin**

2 Kings **2 Kin**

1 Chronicles **1 Chr**

2 Chronicles **2 Chr**

Ezra Ezra

Nehemiah **Neh**

Esther **Esth**

Job Job

Psalms **Ps**

Proverbs **Prov**

Ecclesiastes **Eccl**

Song of Solomon Song

Isaiah **Is**

Jeremiah **Jer**

Lamentations **Lam**

Ezekiel **Ezek**

Daniel **Dan**

Hosea **Hos**

Joel Joel

Amos Amos

Obadiah **Obad**

Jonah **Jon**

Micah **Mic**

Nahum **Nah**

Habakkuk **Hab**

Zephaniah **Zeph**

Haggai **Hag**

Zechariah **Zech**

Malachi **Mal**

Matthew **Matt**

Mark Mark

Luke Luke

John John

Acts Acts

Romans **Rom**

1 Corinthians **1 Cor**

2 Corinthians **2 Cor**

Galatians **Gal**

Ephesians **Eph**

Philippians **Phil**

Colossians **Col**

1 Thessalonians **1 Thess**

2 Thessalonians **2 Thess**

1 Timothy **1 Tim**

2 Timothy **2 Tim**

Titus Titus

Philemon **Philem**

Hebrews **Heb**

James James

1 Peter **1 Pet**

2 Peter **2 Pet**

1 John 1 John

2 John 2 John

3 John 3 John

Jude Jude

Revelation **Rev**

Adapted Scriptures **ADP**

ADDICTIVE SUBSTANCES

Alcohol

Cigarettes

Drugs

Resisting Temptation

Overcoming Addiction

ADDICTIVE SUBSTANCES:

ALCOHOL

The effects of drinking alcohol include:

- Vomiting, liver cirrhosis, cancer, pancreatitis

- Increased irritability, crying, anger, violence

- Slurred speech, blurred vision, staggering gait, confusion, impaired memory, blackouts

- Poor coordination and slow reaction times causing deaths and disabilities by drunk drivers

- Impaired judgment leading to fornication or rape which may result in sexually transmitted diseases, teenage pregnancies and babies with birth defects

- Suicide and injuries from attempted suicide especially in stressed or depressed teens

- Withdrawal symptoms like sweating, morning shakes, confusion, convulsions, hallucination

- Poor academic performance due to hangovers, truancy,

sleeping problems

♦ Misery for the Bible says,

Who has woe?

Who has sorrow?

Who has contentions?

Who has complaints?

Who has wounds without cause?

Who has redness of eyes?

Those who linger long at the wine,

Those who go in search of mixed wine.

Do not look on the wine when it is red,

When it sparkles in the cup,

When it swirls around smoothly;

At the last it bites like a serpent, and stings like a viper. Your eyes will see strange things, and your heart will utter perverse things.

Yes, you will be like one who lies down in the midst of the sea, or like one who lies at the top of the mast saying: "They have struck me, but I was not hurt; they have beaten me, but I did not feel it. When shall I awake, that I may seek another drink?" (Prov 23:29-35)

So abstain from wines, beers, traditional brews, spirits and all other alcoholic drinks because they don't "drown" problems. They compound them with the above complication as they cocoon you in an alcoholic stupor.

ADDICTIVE SUBSTANCES:

CIGARETTES

The effects of smoking cigarettes include:

🚭 Cancer of the lips

🚭 Cancer of the mouth

🚭 Cancer of the throat

🚭 Cancer of the larynx

🚭 Cancer of the lungs

🚭 Cancer of the esophagus

🚭 Cancer of the stomach

🚭 Cancer of the liver

🚭 Cancer of the pancreas

🚭 Cancer of the colon

🚭 Cancer of the kidneys

🚭 Cancer of the bladder

🚭 Cancer of the cervix

🚭 Cough, difficulty breathing, chronic obstructive pulmonary disease

🚭 Heart disease, heart attacks, strokes, blood vessel diseases, gangrene

🚭 Stomach and duodenal ulcers

🚭 Premature aging of the skin, wrinkles, stained fingers

🚭 Stained teeth, gum disease, breath smelling of smoke

🚭 Premature births, small babies and babies with birth defects

ADDICTIVE SUBSTANCES:

DRUGS

The effects of using drugs include:

☠ Cannabinoids (e.g. marijuana): red eyes, impaired thinking, reduced concentration, lack of motivation, withdrawal symptoms e.g. trembling, sweating, diarrhea, vomiting, sleep disturbances

☠ Inhalants (e.g. glue, gasoline, paint thinners): nose bleeding, confusion, permanent brain damage, death

☠ Stimulants (e.g. cocaine, methamphetamine): headaches, high blood pressure, strokes, convulsions, paranoia, death

☠ Depressants (e.g. barbiturates, benzodiazepines): drowsiness, poor coordination, slow heart rate, low blood pressure, coma, death

☠ Narcotics (e.g. morphine, heroin, codeine): drowsiness, depressed breathing, coma, death

☠ Hallucinogens (e.g. Lysergic acid diethylamide LSD): trembling, visual illusions, panic, increased heart rate, high blood pressure, high body temperature

☠ Dissociative anesthetics (e.g. phencyclidine PCP): aggressiveness, disorganized thinking, impaired coordination, sweating, excessive saliva production, convulsions, coma

☠ Club drugs (e.g. Ectasy): euphoria

☠ Others (e.g. anabolic steroids): increased irritability, acne, hair loss, stunted growth, liver disease, stroke, heart attacks.

ADDICTIVE SUBSTANCES:

RESISTING TEMPTATION

Preventing addiction is better than suffering from its ill effects and wasting years of your life and lots of money trying to be free from it.

Therefore, resist the temptation to drink alcohol, smoke cigarettes or use illicit drugs by:

💧🚭☠️Do not continue looking at the temptation for that was Eve's down fall. She ate the illicit fruit because it begun to look delicious and like it could teach her something new for **When the woman saw that the tree was good for food, that it was pleasant to the eyes, and a tree desirable to make one wise, she took of its fruit and ate.** (Gen 3:6)

So, do not continue gazing at the alcohol, drugs or cigarettes because if you do, your perception of them will begin to change. They will begin to look like they can offer you a pleasurable experience that will teach you something new or benefit you in some other way. They will then change from being a definite NO to a MAYBE and finally into a YES. You will then find a reason to justify yielding to the temptation and doing the wrong thing.

⬤🚭☠ Redirect your mind to do the right thing. If Eve had redirected her mind from the devil's words to doing the right thing as per God's words, which were, **You shall not eat it, nor shall you touch it** (Gen 3:3) chances are that she would have never touched the forbidden fruit let alone eaten it.

So, when you are tempted to sip, swallow, sniff, smoke, inject or inhale something you know you should not even touch, instead of thinking about your tempter's words, redirect your mind to doing the right thing and don't touch the addictive substances.

⬤🚭☠ Remind yourself that you can get addicted from your very first sip, sniff or smoke and suffer for the rest of your life. Adam and Eve lost their wonderful life in the Garden of Eden to one of laboring hard for the rest of their lives just because they tasted that one forbidden fruit.

So, do not toy with the idea of trying it just once. Ignore your tempters for they will falsify facts to trick you the way satan, **The serpent deceived Eve by his craftiness** (2 Cor 11:3)

💧🚭☠️ Remind yourself that Adam was punished for eating the banned fruit even though he was served by Eve his wife for **She also gave to her husband with her, and he ate.** (Gen 3:6)

So, don't use drugs, alcohol or cigarettes even if they are given to you by someone you trust like your brother, sister, best friend or closest cousin for you shall reap the negative consequences regardless of who offers them to you.

💧🚭☠️ Remind yourself that despite their excuses, both Adam and Eve were still punished for eating the illicit fruit. Adam's excuse was **The woman whom You gave to be with me, she gave me of the tree** (Gen 3:12) Eve's excuse was **The serpent deceived me** (Gen 3:13)

So understand that excuses and blame shifting will not spare you the negative consequences of using drugs, alcohol or cigarettes.

💧🚭☠️ Remind yourself that what Adam and Eve lost was not worth the taste of that fruit no matter how delicious it was. They lost their idyllic life of lounging while naming animals when they were sent **Out of the garden of Eden to till the ground** (Gen 3:23) and labor hard for the rest of their lives. They also lost their innocence and openness and became guilty and secretive like most drug users, for when God called him, Adam said, **I heard Your voice in the garden, and I was afraid because I was naked; and I hid myself.** (Gen 3:10)

Recognize therefore, that by using addictive substances, you'll loose your idyllic teenage life and become cagey as the addiction tightens its grip on you. You will also loose your good health and spend the rest of your life struggling with chronic sicknesses like cancers, convulsions and cirrhosis. So, don't touch them or taste them.

ADDICTIVE SUBSTANCES:

OVERCOMING ADDICTION

If you have multiple addictions, tackle one addiction at a time. Battle the drugs first, then the alcohol and finally the cigarettes.

To break any addiction, remember the mnemonic STOP

S Set a date to stop.

T Think about why you want to overcome the addiction and write down your reasons. Always carry the paper with you and refer to it when you are tempted to use the addictive substances.

O Omit people and places that encourage you to use addictive substances from your diary.

Ask yourself:

💧🚭☠ Who do I drink/chew/smoke/sniff/ingest/inject myself with?

Then stop spending time with those people.

Do not be deceived: "Evil company corrupts good habits." (1 Cor 15:33) so don't hang out with those who use or praise the use of addictive substances even if you have stopped using them yourself.

Also, **Do not mix with winebibbers, or with gluttonous eaters of meat; for the drunkard and the glutton will come to poverty** (Prov 23:20-21)

💧🚭☠ Where do I drink/chew/smoke/sniff/ inject/ingest the addictive substances?

💧🚭☠ Is it in your home?

Then do not allow the people you used to use the addictive substances with into your home.

💧☹☠ Is it in their homes or dorms?

If so, don't visit them.

💧☹☠ Is it in nightclubs, cafés, hotels or shops?

If so, stay away from those places and avoid the streets where the addictive substances are sold and the boulevards with bars.

In addition, stop going to alcohol drinking parties and do not attend events in smoke filled rooms as you may be tempted to start drinking or smoking again.

💧🚭☠ Put obstacles between you and using the addictive substances by asking yourself:

💧🚭☠ Why do I drink/chew/ smoke/ sniff / inject /ingest the addictive substances?

💧🚭☠ Is it because you are addicted to drugs, alcohol or cigarettes and can't do without them?

If so, seek help from a hospital, doctor or nurse.

💧🚭☠ Is it because the addictive substances are freely available?

If so, decline the free offers like Daniel did during his training for he had free access to alcohol for **The king appointed for them a daily provision of the king's delicacies and of the wine which he drank.** (Dan 1:5)

But he did not drink it for **Daniel purposed in his heart that he would not defile himself with the portion of the king's delicacies, nor with the wine which he drank;** (Dan 1:8)

Decide like Daniel that you will not pollute your body with alcohol, cigarettes or drugs whether or not they are free. Stop accepting free "samples" from "friends" as their aim is to get you hooked so that you can then start paying.

Then go through your room and dorm cubicle and get rid of all alcohol, drugs and cigarettes in your possession.

In addition, do not touch the addictive substances in your home that belong to your parents / guardians.

♦☒☠ Is it so that you can be more comfortable in social situations? If so, see chapter on Shyness.

♦☒☠ Is it because of peer pressure, so that you can socialize with peers using alcohol, cigarettes or drugs?

If so, avoid them even if you have to be alone. Daniel didn't use the excuse that "Most of the other students are drinking and I'll seem weird or antisocial if I don't." He did the right thing and didn't drink the alcohol for it is better to be "anti-social" than to be "anti-God"

Even if all the other students in your learning institution are using addictive substances, you don't have to copy them. Stand firm like Daniel and abstain. See chapters on Negative Peer Pressure and Positive Peer Pressure.

💧🚭☠ When do I drink/chew/smoke/ sniff / inject /ingest the addictive substances?

💧🚭☠ Is it during weekends or school holidays?

If so, use your free time constructively e.g. sing.

💧🚭☠ Is it after listening to certain music?

If so, eject it.

💧🚭☠ Is it when you are stressed?

If so, deal with the specific stressor. Daniel did not justify drinking by saying "I'll drink alcohol to reduce the stress of studying this **Language and literature of the Chaldeans** (Dan 1:4)"

💧🚭☠ Is it when you are lonely or anxious?

If so, see chapters on Loneliness and Anxiety and listen to Christian music, sing and dance.

💧🚭☠ Is it when you can't fall asleep?

If so, read your Bible in bed to calm your mind.

Other things you can do to break free from addictive substances include:

💧🚭☠️ Get saved (see chapter on Jesus Christ). Everyday pray for help to overcome for **He Himself has suffered, being tempted, He is able to aid those who are tempted** (Heb 2:18) Pray even in emergencies when you need strength to overcome strong cravings.

💧🚭☠️ Join a Bible preaching Church, ask your Pastor to pray for you and attend deliverance services.

💧🚭☠️ Remind yourself that **God is faithful, who will not allow you to be tempted beyond what you are able, but with the temptation will also make the way of escape, that you may be able to bear it.** (1 Cor 10:13)

💧🚭☠️ Consult a Christian counselor, doctor or psychologist. Be honest with them so that they can help you. If medications are prescribed, take them faithfully. If you need to be admitted for institutionalized management, cooperate and carry your Bible.

⬥🚫☠ Join a support group like Alcoholics Anonymous (AA) or Narcotics Anonymous (NA) where you will interact with people recovering from similar addictions. If none exists near you, join an online one.

⬥🚫☠ Be patient and persistent in your efforts to stop using the addictive substances. If you start using them again, analyze why you did by going through the 4 steps of STOP, forgive yourself and then stop once again.

⬥🚫☠ Replace the thoughts that encourage you to use addictive substances with Scriptures so that you can start thinking differently. This changing of your mind will help you resist temptation and break free from the addiction.

⬥🚫☠ Read 1 chapter of your Bible daily to learn the Scriptures you'll use to fight the temptation to use addictive substances such us:

⬥🚫☠ Do not be drunk with wine, in which is dissipation. (Eph 5:18)

♦☻⚚Fear the Lord and depart from evil. It will be health to your flesh, and strength to your bones. (Prov 3:7-8)

♦☻⚚Abhor what is evil. Cling to what is good (Rom 12:9)

FAMILY

Family Background

Being an Orphan

Brothers & Sisters

Excessive Responsibilities

Abuse

FAMILY:

FAMILY BACKGROUND

If you don't understand why you were born into a family with many problems, pray for it, **Trust in the Lord with all your heart, and lean not on your own understanding** (Prov 3:5) or lack of it.

As you can't change your birth family, don't waste time comparing it with those of your friends. Use that time to work towards creating the family you would like to have in the future.

E.g. instead of wishing you came to school in a Mercedes Benz instead of a bus, study hard so that you drop your children in your own Benz. As you do so, tell yourself that, *Though my beginning was small, yet my latter end will increase abundantly.* (ADP Job 8:7)

Understand also that you can improve your family situation through prayer for God will hear you just as He heard Ishmael.

After Abraham had sent Ishmael and his mother Hagar away, they wandered in the wilderness until their water got finished and when it seemed that they were to going to die, **God heard the voice of the lad ... Then God opened her eyes, and she saw a well of water.** (Gen 21:17-19)

God heard the voice of Ishmael the lad, and He helped them by showing his mother a well of water, they drew water and didn't die of thirst.

So do not dismiss your prayers as insignificant just because you are young. Pray for your family and God will listen to your prayers just as He heard Ishmael.

Do not also view your contribution to your family's well being as inconsequential for we see that when Pharaoh's daughter found baby Moses in a basket on the riverbank, Miriam, **His sister said to Pharaoh's daughter, "Shall I go and call a nurse for you from the Hebrew women, that she may nurse the child for you?"**

And Pharaoh's daughter said to her, "Go."

So the maiden went and called the child's mother. Then Pharaoh's daughter said to her, "Take this child away and nurse him for me, and I will give you your wages." So the woman took the child and nursed him. (Ex 2:7-9)

Young Miriam cleverly got her mother a job taking care of her own child and so look out for opportunities to help and improve your family's situation.

FAMILY:

BEING AN ORPHAN

Whether your parents died from a disease or an accident or you don't even know what happened to them, don't focus on their absence or waste your life comparing yourself with those who have 2 loving, caring parents.

Focus on God for He is **A father of the fatherless** (Ps 68:5) and learn from Esther that you can succeed in life even if you are an orphan.

Mordecai had brought up Hadassah, that is, Esther, his uncle's daughter, for she had neither father nor mother. (Esth 2:7) She ended up being a Queen, married to King Ahasuerus, **This was the Ahasuerus who reigned over 127 provinces from, India to Ethiopia** (Esth 1:1)

So don't limit your aspirations just because you don't have earthy parents. Pray to your heavenly Father, work hard, obey your earthly guardians and you will be successful like her.

Esther obeyed the command of Mordecai as when she was brought up by him. (Esth 2:20) Her obedience combined with prayer and fasting enabled her to save the lives of the Jews in the 127 provinces under King Ahasuerus. For this great feat, a whole book of the Bible written about her and we remember her today.

Therefore, pray and obey, be confident and courageous and your heavenly Father will help you accomplish great things in life even if you are an orphan.

FAMILY:
BROTHERS & SISTERS

If your brothers or sisters are stressing you, stay faithful to God and He will change your situation from one full of stress into one full of blessings like He did for Joseph and David.

Joseph's brothers stressed him for they sold him into slavery because they were jealous of him. However, he remained faithful to God through many years of suffering and God turned his stressful situation into one full of blessings such that the next time they met, **Joseph recognized his brothers, but they did not recognize him** (Gen 42:8) for he was not a slave, but Pharaoh's Deputy governing Egypt for Pharaoh had said to him, **I have set you over all the land of Egypt.** (Gen 41:41)

David's brother also stressed him by publicly insulting him when he heard David asking about the reward for killing Goliath. **Now Eliab his oldest brother heard when he spoke to the men; and Eliab's anger was aroused against David, and he said, "Why did you come down here? And with whom have you left those few sheep in the wilderness?**

I know your pride and the insolence of your heart, for you have come down to see the battle." (1 Sam 17:28)

And David said, "What have I done now? (1 Sam 17:29) By asking this, it shows that this wasn't the first time that his brother berated him.

David then continued, Is there not a cause?" Then he turned from him toward another (1 Sam 17:28-30) That is what you should do when your siblings or other people try to restrict your aspirations by demeaning you. Turn away from them and do not let their sour expressions stop you from pursuing your goals. Close your ears to their caustic words, believe in God and in yourself, do your best and you will achieve great things like David who killed Goliath despite his brother contemptibly underestimating his abilities.

If on the other hand your siblings stress you by using your clothes and other belongings without your permission, be the mature one. Speak to them nicely and ask them to stop doing it.

If they ignore you, report them to your parents/ guardians and see that justice is done. If nothing is done, and they refuse to change, then pray for strength to live with them as you work very hard so that one day you will be able to move out into your own place where no one will touch your things without your consent.

FAMILY:
EXCESSIVE RESPONSIBILITIES

If you are stressed by the many responsibilities and chores you have to do at home because they leave you too tired or with very little time to study, ask your parents to reduce them. If they refuse, make the best use of your time in school.

Revise and do your homework during your tea and lunch breaks and when the teacher is late for a lesson. Pay attention in class to grasp all that is taught. On your way home, whether you are walking or in a bus, go through what you were taught that day while it is still fresh in your mind.

Don't waste a precious moment playing with students who have time to study at home. Do your very best and God will bless your efforts.

FAMILY:

ABUSE

Is anyone among you suffering? Let him pray. (James 5:13) Regardless of whether relatives or family workers are abusing you physically, verbally, mentally or sexually, if you are suffering, ask God to help you for He says **Call upon Me in the day of trouble; I will deliver you** (Ps 50:15)

You can pray, **I ... cry out to God Most High ... He shall send from heaven and save me; God shall send forth His mercy and His truth.** (Ps 57:2-3)

Then tell the abuser to stop abusing you. If you can't tell them in the face for whatever reason, or if they ignore you and continue abusing you, tell a trustworthy person your problems.

Your confidant may talk to the abuser on your behalf, suggest solutions, support you emotionally and you'll begin to feel better even if your situation hasn't changed. You can talk to:

🏛 Your Parents or other Relatives

E.g. grandparents, aunties or older cousins

🏛 A Family friend

E.g. your parents' friends or neighbors

🏛 A Pastor

Open your heart to a Pastor or a church leader.

🏛 A Teacher

Share with one teacher your problems.

🏛 A Counselor

Get counseling preferably from a Christian counselor.

🏛 A Doctor

Get treatment for mental and physical illnesses.

🏛 A Lawyer

For legal aid. See chapter on Helpful Numbers.

🏛 A Social Worker

Visit the Children's Department for advice.

🏛 Children's Home Staff

They'll help you or refer you to a social worker.

🏛 Non Governmental Organizations NGO's)

Seek aid from NGO's and charitable groups. See chapter on Helpful Numbers.

🏛 Your Chief

Tell them your problems and heed their advice.

After you have done all that you can about your abusive situation, you now have to persevere as you patiently wait for God to do for you what you cannot do for yourself.

As you wait on God, focus on His immense power and not on the immensity of your problems. If the abusive situation worsens, intensify your prayers like Jesus who **Being in agony, He prayed more earnestly.** (Luke 22:44)

Keep your mind on God so that you will be at peace for His Word promises us that **You will keep him in perfect peace, whose mind is stayed on You, because he trusts in You.** (Is 26:3)

Meditate also on Scriptures like these and the oppressive actions arising from your abusive situation will not be able to depress you:

🏛 **In Me You may have peace. In the world you will have tribulation; but be of good cheer, I have overcome the world.** (John 16:33)

🏛 **Many are the afflictions of the righteous, but the Lord delivers him out of them all.** (Ps 34:19)

🏛 *My Redeemer is strong; the Lord of hosts is His name. He will thoroughly plead my case* (ADP Jer 50:34)

FEELINGS & EMOTIONS

Anger

Anxiety & Worry

Confusion

Fear

Feeling Inadequate

Feeling like Giving Up

Feeling Unloved

Guilt

Loneliness

Love & Lust

Low Self-Confidence

Revenge

Sadness

Shyness

FEELINGS:

ANGER

When someone tries to ignite the flames of ire in you, remember that **He who is slow to anger is better than the mighty, and he who rules his spirit than he who takes a city.** (Prov 16:32)

Try to ignore the trigger for **The discretion of a man makes him slow to anger, and his glory is to overlook a transgression.** (Prov 19:11)

If you do get infuriated, **Be angry, and do not sin** (Eph 4:26) or make a decision when you are mad (pun intended).

Do not let the sun go down on your wrath. (Eph 4:26) Douse it with deep breaths or stroll away to saturate your heart with soothing music.

Do not let it simmer inside you **For anger rests in the**

bosom of fools (Eccl 7:9) before it burns them.

Avoid dealing with angry people for **A wrathful man stirs up strife, but he who is slow to anger allays contention.** (Prov 15:18) If you are dealing with one and they loose their temper, keep quiet until they calm down. If they fly into a rage, walk away before they hit the ceiling. Return once they have cooled down (if you have to).

Finally, **Make no friendship with an angry man, and with a furious man do not go, lest you learn his ways and set a snare for your soul.** (Prov 22:24-25)

FEELINGS:

ANXIETY & WORRY

Jesus asked, **Which of you by worrying can add one cubit to his stature?** (Luke 12:25)

No one can solve any problem whether physical, mental, social or financial by worrying.

For worry entangles your mind in a web of "What ifs?" e.g. What if I fail? What if I get sick? What if I don't get a college? What if I am robbed? So, don't waste your time worrying.

Instead, **Be anxious for nothing, but in everything by prayer and supplication, with thanksgiving, let your requests be made known to God; and the peace of God, which surpasses all understanding, will guard your hearts and minds through Christ Jesus.** (Phil 4: 6-7)

Set aside time every day to pray. Write down all your worrisome challenges and ask God to help you as you think of possible solutions.

Write down the possible solutions and create an action plan for each solution. Then begin working on your action plan to solve your problem instead of worrying about it.

For those challenges that you can't think of a possible solution, the action plan is to forward them to God in prayer and trustingly leave them in His capable hands.

Trust that God will take care of them and you will disentangle your mind from the web of worry for trusting God is the antidote to worrying.

FEELINGS:

CONFUSION

In you are confused about anything, pray to The Lord of hosts, who is wonderful in counsel and excellent in guidance. (Is 28:29)

Seek His counsel for If any of you lacks wisdom, let him ask of God, who gives to all liberally and without reproach, and it will be given to him. (James 1:5)

You can pray, Cause me to know the way in which I should walk, for I lift up my soul to You. (Ps 143:8)

Then read your Bible everyday To know wisdom and instruction,

to perceive the words of understanding,

to receive the instruction of wisdom, justice, judgment and equity; (Prov 1:2-3)

This will enable you to find your way and live life in an orderly and organized manner even if you have no reliable human to guide you. It will also save you from wasting years correcting the chaos caused by the errors of your youth.

In addition, don't look for help from fortune tellers, palm readers or daily stars to chart your way out of a state of confusion for you will get more lost as you compound the confusion with sin.

FEELINGS:

FEAR

Fight fear because it tortures you.

When you are constantly frightened of failing exams, scared you won't get into the college of your choice, petrified of being mugged, afraid you won't get a good job or terrified you won't afford food or fare or fuel you are torturing yourself for **Fear involves torment.** (1 John 4:18)

Therefore fight it aggressively **For God has not given us a spirit of fear, but of power** (2 Tim 1:7)

Fight fear by having faith in God. If people or situations try to frighten you, say to yourself:

✞ The Lord is my helper; I will not fear. (Heb 13: 6)

✞ The Lord is on my side; I will not fear. (Ps 118:6)

✝The Lord is the strength of my life; of whom shall I be afraid? (Ps 27:1)

Believe that the Lord is on your side, He is your Helper and the Strength of your life and you will not have a reason to fear anyone or anything.

Then do your best and leave the rest to God as you confidently march into your future believing that **Though I walk through the valley of the shadow of death, I will fear no evil, for You are with me** (Ps 23:4)

FEELINGS:

FEELING INADEQUATE

When you feel weak, inadequate or overwhelmed, pray to God for **He gives power to the weak, and to those who have no might He increases strength.** (Is 40:29)

You can say: *Strengthen me with might through Your Spirit in the inner man.* (ADP Eph 3:16)

Then ask those around you to help you. If they refuse or are unable to do so, do your best while believing that God's help is enough for He says **My strength is made perfect in weakness.** (2 Cor 12:9) This means that God's great strength is perfectly displayed when it is working through our human weakness for we are then able to achieve great things.

David may have seemed weak to the lions, bears and Goliath but with God's help, he was able to destroy all of them. So never back down from gigantic problems even if you are alone for

You + God = The Winning Team.

Face your challenges confidently and you will overcome them if you do your best while believing that:

✝ God is my strength and power (2 Sam 22:33)

✝ I can do all things through Christ who strengthens me. (Phil 4:13)

✝ The people who know their God shall be strong, and carry out great exploits. (Dan 11:32)

FEELINGS:

FEELING LIKE GIVING UP

Never give up even if you are all alone in your stressful situation. Learn from Joseph, who didn't despair, even when no human could help him out of his stressful situation when he was imprisoned after been falsely accused of rape by the wife of Potiphar, who was **An officer of Pharaoh, captain of the guard** (Gen 39:1).

Joseph's father could not help him as he thought was dead. His brothers could not help him as they were the ones who had sold him into slavery and cheated their father that he was dead.

His last hope for human help had been the chief butler whose dream he had interpreted for Joseph had said to him, **But remember me when it is well with you, and please show kindness to me; make mention of me to Pharaoh, and get me out of this house. For indeed I ... have done nothing here that they should put me into the dungeon.** (Gen 40:14-15)

Nevertheless, after he was released, **The chief butler did not remember Joseph, but forgot him.** (Gen 40:23) However, God did not forget Joseph and He has not forgotten you.

2 years after the chief butler was released, Pharaoh dreamt a dream that none of his wise men could interpret. This reminded the chief butler of Joseph's correct interpretation of his own dream. He told Pharaoh about him **Then Pharaoh sent and called Joseph, and they brought him quickly out of the dungeon** (Gen 41:14)

Joseph interpreted his dream and Pharaoh said, **You shall be over my house, and all my people shall be ruled according to your word ... I have set you over all the land of Egypt.** (Gen 41:40-41)

So never give up no matter how humanly hopeless your stressful situation is for you don't know how God will intervene to help you out.

To avoid drowning in despair, always believe that one day, you will experience God's goodness like David who said, **I would have lost heart, unless I had believed that I would see the goodness of the Lord in the land of the living.** (Ps 27:13)

Never give up on God even if you have given up on people. Do your best to help yourself like Joseph who asked the chief butler for help and then wait on God to do the rest for you.

As you wait on God, do not let your waiting period be your worrying period. Wait while believing that God will come through for you and meditate on these Scriptures to avoid giving in to the darkness of despair.

- Unto the upright there arises light in the darkness. (Ps 112:4)

- Is anything too hard for the Lord? (Gen 18:14)

- With God nothing will be impossible. (Luke 1:37)

FEELINGS:

FEELING UNLOVED

If you don't feel loved, know that *God so loved* (your name) *that He gave His only begotten Son, that if I believe in Him I shall not perish but have everlasting life.* (ADP John 3:16)

Know that neither stressful situations or sorrow or persecution or poverty or defenselessness or danger or war can separate you from God's love for **His compassions fail not.** (Lam 3:22)

If you don't feel His love for you, pray,

Cause me to hear Your lovingkindness in the morning, for in You do I trust. (Ps 143:8)

Then resolve to love yourself by doing one kind thing for yourself everyday as you meditate on these Scriptures:

♥ **The Lord will command His lovingkindness in the daytime, and in the night His song shall be with me.** (Ps 42:8)

♥ The Lord has appeared of old to me, saying: "Yes I have loved you with an everlasting love; therefore with loving kindness I have drawn you" (Jer 31:3)

♥ I am persuaded that neither death nor life, nor angels nor principalities nor powers, nor things present nor things to come, nor height nor depth, nor any other created thing, shall be able to separate us from the love of God which is in Christ Jesus our Lord. (Rom 8:38-39)

FEELINGS:

GUILT

If you are feeling guilty, confess your sins to God for **If we confess our sins, He is faithful and just to forgive us our sins and to cleanse us from all unrighteousness.** (1 John 1:9)

You can pray, **Do not remember the sins of my youth, nor my transgressions; according to Your mercy remember me, for Your goodness sake, O Lord.** (Ps 25:7) Then receive God's forgiveness and forgive yourself.

Apologize to those you hurt, compensate them for any damages and get saved (see chapter on Jesus Christ) for **If anyone is in Christ, he is a new creation; old things have passed away; behold, all things have become new.** (2 Cor 5:17)

Since you are now a new creation who has left their old mistakes behind, every time the guilty thoughts come into your mind remind yourself that **There is therefore now no condemnation to those who are in Christ Jesus.** (Rom 8:1)

If people try to make you feel guilty about your past forgiven sins, tell yourself that **As far as the east is from the west, so far has He removed our transgressions from us.** (Ps 103:12)

In addition, you should not condemn other people for **Who are you to judge another?** (James 4:12)

The Lord will judge His people (Heb 10:30) not you or me.

FEELINGS:
LONELINESS

When you feel lonely, remind yourself that God is with you for **He Himself has said, "I will never leave you nor forsake you."** (Heb 13:5)

Phone him by praying for He promises, **Call to Me, and I will answer you** (Jer 33:3).

You can pray, **Look on my right hand and see, for there is no one who acknowledges me; refuge has failed me; no one cares for my soul ... Attend to my cry, for I am brought very low.** (Ps 142:4-6)

Even if all your family and friends have deserted you, know that God is still with you for as David declared **When my father and my mother forsake me, then the Lord will take care of me.** (Ps 27:10)

FEELINGS:

LOVE & LUST

If you are wondering whether what you are feeling is love or lust, use this checklist which uses the definition of love in 1 Cor 13:4-8.

♥ Love suffers long.

Love is patient and able to wait for the right time, place and circumstances to do everything the right way.

Lust is impatient. It wants to have its way without delay regardless of the repercussions. It cannot wait for tomorrow let alone to finish school.

♥ Love ... is kind

Lust is unkind. It will use blackmail or threats to terminate the relationship or other mean means to get what it wants.

♥ Love does not envy

Lust is envious.

♥ Love ... is not puffed up

Lust is conceited and proud.

♥ Love ... does not behave rudely

Love respects the object of its affection, their relatives and friends.

Lust is bad mannered.

♥ Love ... does not seek its own

Love seeks the good of all concerned parties. It considers the other person's feelings before it does anything as it does not want to hurt them.

Lust is selfish as it just seeks to satisfy itself. It will pressurize one to do things detrimental to their health, education and future to gratify itself.

♥ Love ... is not provoked

Lust is easily irritated.

♥ Love ... thinks no evil

Lust thrives on dirty thoughts and records how it has been wronged.

♥ Love ... does not rejoice in iniquity

Love does the right thing before God and man. Lust enjoys sinning.

♥ Love...rejoices in the truth

Lust thrives on lies.

♥ Love ... bears all things

Love cherishes and cares during both happy and sad times. It matures as a result of the joys and sorrows experienced by the couple together.

Lust breaks easily under the strain of problems and gives up on the relationship. It does not have the heart to hang around when trouble comes as it just wants its needs to be met quickly and not to deal with tribulations.

♥ Love ... endures all things

Love perseveres through stressful periods in the relationship and in life.

Lust does not persevere for long during difficult times. It abandons easily, ending the relationship.

♥ Love never fails

Love stands the test of time. It can love one person for decades.

Lust is fleeting and fails the test of time. One day it can be in lust with one person and the next it can be in lust with a different person.

FEELINGS:

LOW SELF CONFIDENCE & LOW SELF ESTEEM

If you have little confidence in yourself and in your abilities, you will accomplish little in life for how you perceive yourself determines what you achieve for yourself.

We see that the Israelites initially were unable to conquer the Promised Land because they had a low opinion of themselves for they said, **There we saw the giants ... and we were like grasshoppers in our own sight.** (Num 13:33)

As they saw themselves as grasshoppers going to fight against giants, their low self-confidence and low confidence in God's ability to help them prolonged their suffering in the wilderness.

Therefore, have gigantic confidence in God's ability to help you and great confidence in your own abilities and you will defeat gigantic problems and achieve great things in life.

If you have low confidence in yourself, increase it by recalling what the Bible says about you:

☺ You are a child of God

I will be a Father to you, and you shall be My sons and daughters, says the Lord Almighty. (2 Cor 6:18)

☺ You are a wonderfully made

I am fearfully and wonderfully made. (Ps 139:14)

☺ You are a conqueror

In all these things we are more than conquerors through Him who loved us. (Rom 8:37)

Every morning say to yourself:

I am a wonderfully created child of God and in all these challenges I am more than a conqueror through Jesus Christ who loves me.

Repeat it whenever you face a problem to affirm to yourself that you can overcome it with God's help.

Combine this with thinking highly of yourself for you are God's child because if you were the King's child you would think highly of yourself just because you were born into that family.

Consistently think good thoughts about yourself and as your thoughts change for the better, your feelings about yourself will also improve and you will begin to feel good about yourself and develop healthy self-confidence.

If someone calls you ugly, useless, unwanted, a grasshopper or any other belittling adjective or noun, say to yourself:

I am a wonderfully created child of God and in all these challenges I am more than a conqueror through Jesus Christ who loves me.

Repeat it and believe it and you will find that in time, no person will be able to lower your self confidence.

If their insults hurt you, do something that will make you feel better. E.g. listen to music, draw, or sing. Do something constructive and not destructive so that you do not lower yourself to the level where your mockers want to keep you.

Other things that you can do improve your self-confidence include:

☻ Count your blessings instead of counting your problems for each blessing is a reason to feel good about yourself and life.

1. Personal blessings

Do you have a creative brain or an artistic flair or musical ears or a melodious voice or smooth skin or strong arms or cute toes or a pumping heart? Thank God for every part of your body.

2. Family blessings

Do you have a helpful father or a caring mother or a protective brother or a kind sister or gentle grandparents or concerned cousins? Thank God for each of your relatives and friends.

3. Other blessings

Do you have clothes to wear or food to eat or a place to call home or a school to attend?

Thank God for all your blessings.

☺ Write down 10 things you like about yourself or others like about you. For example: 1. I passed last terms exams with flying colors

2. I am obedient to my parents

3. I am a loyal friend

4. I write good English essays

5. I do not steal

6. I can cook chicken very well

7. I have a healthy hair

8. I am an eloquent debater

9. I am a fast swimmer

10. I am the fastest sprinter in my class

Carry your list with you to help you value and respect yourself more as it will remind you of your good points and successes. Keep adding to this list whenever you accomplish something else outstanding.

🙂 Perfect one of your talents by improving your skills.

For example if you write middling English essays, read classical novels and practice writing until you are the best in your class. If you are an average basketball player, watch great players playing and practice shooting three pointers until you are the highest scorer.

If you play the guitar satisfactorily, practice until you win awards at the music festival. If you grow unremarkable tomatoes, research and improve your techniques until you produce the largest in your locality.

Hone your skills and as you begin to excel, your confidence in that ability will increase and this new found confidence will boost your general self confidence.

☻ Join and participate in a group activity like a choir, drama club or football team. Being an active member of the group will increase your self confidence especially as the group increases its trust in you and gives you more responsibilities.

☻ Exercise regularly and you will regularly feel good since your body releases endorphins that make you feel good when you exercise. Regular exercise also improves your self-esteem by improving your appearance as your skin glows and your muscles get toned.

☻ Improve personal hygiene by keeping your hair neat, nails tidy and using a deodorant.

☻ Improve your dressing. See chapter on Fashion.

FEELINGS:

REVENGE

Do not avenge yourselves, but rather give place to wrath; for it is written, "Vengeance is Mine, I will repay," says the Lord. (Rom 12:19)

Do not say, "I will recompense evil"; wait for the Lord, and He will save you. (Prov 20:22)

Pray, O Lord of Hosts, You Who judge righteously...let me see Your vengeance on them, for to You I have revealed my cause. (Jer 11:20)

Then focus on your studies and Do not rejoice when your enemy falls, and do not let your heart be glad when he stumbles; lest the Lord see it, and it displease Him, and He turn away His wrath from him. (Prov 24:17-18)

FEELINGS:
SADNESS

When you feel sad and want to cry, do not be afraid to do so as it is not a sign of weakness for even **Jesus wept.** (John 11:35)

Sob and you'll feel better after releasing the pent up tension and toxins through your tears.

Then pray for God says, **I, even I, am He who comforts you.** (Is 51:12)

You can pray, **Hear my prayer, O Lord ... for the enemy has persecuted my soul; he has crushed my life to the ground; he has made me dwell in darkness, like those who have long been dead. Therefore my spirit is overwhelmed within me; my heart within me is distressed ... revive me O Lord for your name's sake.** (Ps 143:1-11)

Then ascertain why you are sad by asking yourself **Why are you cast down, O my soul? And why are you disquieted within me?**

Hope in God; For I shall yet praise Him, the help of my countenance and my God. (Ps 42:11)

If you are sad because of problems, **Cast your burden on the Lord, and He shall sustain you** (Ps 55: 22) and the problems won't depress you.

If it is because of something you did, know that **Godly sorrow produces repentance leading to salvation, not to be regretted** (2 Cor 7:10). Ask God to forgive you and forgive yourself.

If you are sad because you lack something, prayerfully **Ask, and you will receive, that your joy maybe full.** (John 16:24)

Then sing praises and meditate on these Scriptures to lift your spirit:

☺ I **Shall obtain joy and gladness; sorrow and sighing shall flee away.** (Is 51:11)

☺ **God, who comforts the downcast, comforted us** (2 Cor 7:6)

☺ This is the day the Lord has made; we will rejoice and be glad in it. (Ps 118:24)

If you usually feel like crying, record the tear triggering situations in a book so that you can avoid them or manage them more effectively.

If you are always tearful, consult a doctor as you may be depressed. Take your medications and pray, **I am weary with my crying; ... My prayer is to You, O Lord ... hear me in the truth of Your salvation. Deliver me out of the mire, and let me not sink** (Ps 69:3-14) in depression.

FEELINGS:

SHYNESS

Shyness stresses you by restraining you when you want to talk to people or do things publicly. To overcome it, pray for strength to break free from it and then go out and meet people.

Join a choir, youth club or team sport such as basketball and you will make friends with your colleagues as you practice together.

If you want to talk to a specific person, smile at them on your first encounter.

The next time you meet them:

1) Smile

2) Greet them with a simple "Hi!" or "Sasa?"

The 3rd time you run into them:

1) Smile

2) Greet them

3) Compliment them by saying something good and truthful about them. E.g. "You have a nice outfit" OR "You have a nice shoes" OR "I like your hairstyle". Make them feel nice about themselves and they'll respond positively to you.

The 4th time you bump into them:

1) Smile

2) Greet them

3) Compliment them

4) Ask them one simple question that demands an answer. E.g. "Where are you going?" OR "What time is it?" Don't question them about their private life or bombard them with questions.

The 5th time you meet them:

1) Smile

2) Greet them

3) Compliment them

4) Ask them several question as you strike up a conversation. E.g. "Where are you going?" AND "By the way, what is your name?" OR "What time is it?" AND "Where do you live?"

If you know their interests, ask about them. If you don't know them, ask them about general things like school, sports, movies or music. If they answer your questions, listen to their answers and let the conversation flow from there.

If they ignore you, laugh or ridicule you, do not take it to heart or let it keep you from meeting other people. Move on and find another person whom you can practice the above steps on until you conquer shyness completely.

FRIENDS:

Negative Peer Pressure

Positive Peer Pressure

True & False Friends

High Expectations from Friends

How to Relax with Friends

Opposite Sex Relationships

Broken Relationships

FRIENDS:
NEGATIVE PEER PRESSURE

Negative peer pressure occurs when other youth coerce you to do something with negative consequences like taking drugs, drinking alcohol, smoking cigarettes, watching pornography, having premarital sex or committing crimes such as stealing or burning school property.

They can apply the pressure by asking you to prove yourself by doing something.

E.g. "If you really love me, let's do this" or "If you are a real man/lady do it". Know that this is the tactic the devil used to tempt Jesus for he said, **If You are the Son of God,** do ... (Matt 4:3, 6) Resist the pressure by living to please God like Jesus and you won't be pressured into sin by the need to please others or prove yourself to them.

Peers can also negatively pressurize you by boasting that they have done that activity even if they haven't. They brag to make you feel inexperienced for not having done it.

If they brag about engaging in negative activities to make you feel inferior, feel superior for not having succumbed to the negativity.

They can also pressure you verbally with insults.

E.g. They may call you "chicken" or "coward" for refusing to engage in negative activities.

If they do so, ignore them, for their insults won't land you in a mortuary, hospital or jail.

Peers can apply pressurize with sugary words.

E.g. They may tell you that you are very beautiful or that they love you very much and want to demonstrate their strong love for you.

If they use flattery, remind yourself of the bitter consequences of their sweet words.

They can also pressurize you with lies about the consequences of those activities.

E.g. They may say, "It's a safe drug" or "Once won't hurt".

Read the chapters on Alcohol, Cigarettes, Drugs, Stopping Sexual Sin and Crime so that you won't believe their lies.

Peers can also pressure you with their actions by performing the negative behaviour e.g. smoking in your presence to lure you to engage in it as well.

If sinners entice you, do not consent (Prov 1:10) Leave immediately they begin doing so.

They can also pressure you by giving you gifts.

E.g. They may buy you chocolates or clothes and then insist you to engage in premarital sex as your way of thanking them.

If they spend money on you, spend some on them too or split the bills. If you don't have money to spend on them, then refuse their gifts.

In addition, know that pressurizers can be very persistent and exposing yourself to their persistent pressure can break you.

Learn from Samson who was destroyed after Delilah **Pestered him daily with her words and pressed him, so that his soul was vexed to death, that he told her all his heart**(Judg 16:16) She then acted quickly and reduced the strongest man in the land to a blind grinder in the prison.

So avoid all negative peers so that they don't break you and help you mess your life.

Understand also, that even as a teenager, you can resist negative pressure from adults. Learn from Daniel's 3 friends who refused to buckle to the king's negative pressure and bow down to his idol even after he threatened to throw them into a flaming furnace.

For Shadrach, Meshach, and Abed-Nego answered and said to the king,

"O Nebuchadnezzar, we have no need to answer you in this matter. If that is the case, our God whom we serve is able to deliver us from the burning fiery furnace, and He will deliver us from your hand, O king. But if not, let it be known to you, O king, that we do not serve your gods, nor will we worship the gold image you which you have set up." (Dan 3:16-18)

Likewise, you can say to the adults who are negatively pressurizing you, "I will not steal or smoke or engage in premarital sex or any other negative behaviour because God does not want me to do so." Then leave the situation.

If you can't leave the situation physically, leave it mentally by praying. If you have to suffer dire consequences know that God will help you as He helped the 3 friends for the King said **I see four men loose, walking in the midst of the fire; and they are not hurt, and the form of the fourth is like the Son of God.** (Dan 3:25)

Finally, don't negatively pressurize your peers for **Whoever causes the upright to go astray in an evil way, he himself will fall into his own pit** (Prov 28:10)

Don't mislead even those younger than you for **Whoever causes one of these little ones who believe in Me to sin, it would be better for him if a millstone was hung around his neck, and he were drowned in the depths of the sea.** (Matt 18:6)

FRIENDS:

POSITIVE PEER PRESSURE

Positive peer pressure occurs when other youth compel you to do things with positive outcomes like passing exams or abstaining from sex.

Spend time with friends who exert positive pressure on you with their actions or words so that you can resist negative peer pressure.

To differentiate positive from negative pressure and help you decide if you should succumb or resist it, listen to your parents and teachers and read one chapter of your Bible every day so that you can know what God would like you to do in each and every situation.

In addition, exert positive pressure to teens who are sliding into the destruction of alcohol, drugs, cigarettes and premarital sex for you are to **Deliver those who are drawn** to death, and hold back those who are stumbling to the slaughter.

If you say, "Surely we did not know this," does not He who weighs the hearts consider it?

He who keeps your soul, does He not know it? And will He not render to each man according to his deeds? (Prov 24:11-12)

Therefore, since God is watching and He knows when you can do something to help someone without endangering your own life, ask Him to guide you as you help at risk teens.

FRIENDS:

TRUE & FALSE FRIENDS

The righteous should choose his friends carefully, for the way of the wicked leads them astray. (Prov 12:26)

So choose friends who believe in Jesus Christ and Do not be unequally yoked together with unbelievers. For what fellowship has righteousness with lawlessness?

And what communion has light with darkness? And what accord has Christ with Belial?

Or what part a believer with an unbeliever?

And what agreement has the temple of God with idols?

For you are the temple of the living God. (2 Cor 6:14-16)

Choose your friends carefully and learn from David and Jonathan who are the perfect example of true friendship.

Jonathan was a faithful friend for when David's life was in

danger, **Jonathan told David, saying, "My father Saul seeks to kill you. Therefore please be on your guard."** (1 Sam 19:2)

Then **Jonathan spoke well of David to Saul his father** (1 Sam 19:4) and King Saul said he would not kill David.

King Saul later changed his mind but Jonathan helped David again for he said, "**If it pleases my father to do you evil, then I will report it to you and send you away, that you may go in safety.** (1 Sam 20:13)

Jonathan then went and asked King Saul what David had done that he deserved to die and **Saul cast a spear at him to kill him, by which Jonathan knew that it was determined by his father to kill David.** (1 Sam 20:33) He then went and warned David using the secret code they had developed and David left the city.

David also proved to be a faithful friend to Jonathan for after Jonathan and his father Saul had died **David said, "Is there still anyone who is left of the house of Saul, that I may show him kindness for Jonathan's sake?"** (2 Sam 9:1)

They then brought Mephibosheth, who was disabled, to him and **David said to him, "Do not fear, for I will surely show you kindness for Jonathan your father's sake, and will restore to you all the land of Saul your grandfather; and you shall eat bread at my table continually.** (2 Sam 9:7)

Thus David and Jonathan teach us that true friendships does not end with death for your true friends will take care of your interests after you die just as they took care of you when you were alive. Therefore, **Do not forsake your own friend or your father's friend** (Prov 27:10)

Their friendship also teaches us that **Confidence in an unfaithful man in time of trouble is like a bad tooth and a foot out of joint.** (Prov 25:19) For if David had relied on an unfaithful friend when King Saul was trying to kill him, he may have died.

So identify your true friends early so that when you get in trouble, you will know who to rely on. Do not depend on false friends as trying to walk out of a problem with their help is like trying to walk on a dislocated leg that slows your progress and causes you severe pain every step you take.

To differentiate your true friends from the false ones, heed the Bible which says:

👥 **A friend loves at all times** (Prov 17:17) True friends will be with you during the good times and the bad times when you have problems. Jonathan stuck with David when he was a hero and when he was hiding in the field for his life.

👥 **A man who has friends must himself be friendly, but there is a friend who sticks closer than a brother.** (Prov 18:24) True friends will help you even when your brothers and sisters cannot help you. Jonathan helped David even when his own brothers were not there to help him.

👥 **A talebearer reveals secrets, but he who is of a faithful spirit conceals a matter.** (Prov 11:13) A true friend won't divulge your secrets. Jonathan didn't disclose David's hiding place.

👥 **The sweetness of a man's friend gives delight by hearty counsel.** (Prov 27:9) True friends give you good advice. Listen to it even if it hurts for **Faithful are the wounds of a friend, but the kisses of the enemy are deceitful.** (Prov 27:6) False friends butter you with lies **Therefore do not associate with one who flatters with his lips.** (Prov 20:19)

As iron sharpens iron, so a man sharpens the countenance of his friends. (Prov 27:17) True friends enlighten you for **He who walks with wise men will be wise, but the companion of fools will be destroyed.** (Prov 13:20) So pick friends who don't spread rumors or make fun of doing the wrong thing for **Whoever spreads slander is a fool** (Prov 10:18) and **Fools mock at sin** (Prov 14:9).

FRIENDS:

HIGH EXPECTATIONS FROM FRIENDS

If your friends expect too much from you e.g. they want you to wear the hottest outfits or own the latest phone even if your parents can't afford them, don't let their expectations pressure you to engage in immoral or illegal activities to acquire those items.

Do not try to live up to standards that you cannot maintain because it will stress you and your "friends" will see through your hypocrisy. They will drop you and you will end up having gone through a lot of trouble for nothing.

Understand that true friends will accept you just as you are so do not waste your time and energy tying to fit in where you do not really fit in.

Accept Jesus' invitation for He loves you just as you are and take off the heavy yoke of trying to live up to other peoples' expectations.

Take His yoke (i.e. His rules for living) and live only to please Him and you will find the peaceful rest that earthly friends can never give you for He says, **Come to Me, all you who labor and are heavy laden, and I will give you rest. Take My yoke upon you and learn from Me, for I am gentle and lowly in heart, and you will find rest for your souls. For My yoke is easy and My burden is light.** (Matt 11:28-30)

FRIENDS:

HOW TO RELAX WITH FRIENDS

🚲 Listen to good music from CDs, tapes or the radio. Alternatively, compose it as you rap, **Speaking to one another in psalms and hymns and spiritual songs, singing and making melody in your heart to the Lord.** (Eph 5:19)

🚲 Watch comedy DVD's, videos or TV shows and share jokes or funny stories since laughter relieves tension and reduces stress hormones and **A merry heart does good, like medicine.** (Prov 17:22).

🚲 Bask in the sun as exposure to sunlight raises the levels of serotonin and this can impart feelings of calmness and emotional well-being.

🚲 Exercise in group sports like basketball.

🚲 Shop or just window shopping

🚲 Rear rabbits or grow vegetables for nature helps one relax and you'll also generate money.

🚲 Study the Bible together and strengthen your faith for faith is an effective stress reducer.

🚲 Assist the less fortunate e.g. Helping out in a children's home for you will appreciate your blessings better and God will bless you for **Blessed is he who considers the poor; the Lord will deliver him in time of trouble. The Lord will preserve Him and keep him alive, and he will be blessed on the earth ... The Lord will strengthen him on his bed of illness** (Ps 41:1-3)

FRIENDS:
OPPOSITE SEX RELATIONSHIPS

During your teenage years avoid serious relationships with members of the opposite sex and have serious relationships with your books.

Socialize with other teenagers in group settings as you get to know yourself and understand the opposite sex better. You can study together, watch movies, hike, or have picnics.

As you mingle, view the members of the opposite sex as potential good friends and not as potential boyfriends or girlfriends. Treat them respectfully as this will foster strong friendships and you will also avoid embarrassing yourself as you try to impress them.

If you are very fond of a particular member of the opposite sex, take your time to know them and ensure you like them first as a friend before the relationship can grow to one of loving each other and when it does, don't engage in premarital sex.

If one party is only interested in the sex and they realize that they are not going to get it until they marry you, then they will reconsider staying around and they may end the relationship.

This is good for the party that loves genuinely for it is better to be dumped when you don't have sexually transmitted illnesses and a guilty conscience than to be dumped with both plus a broken heart and shattered self respect.

FRIENDS:

BROKEN RELATIONSHIPS

To get over a broken relationship, ask God to heal your pain for **He heals the brokenhearted and binds up their wounds.** (Ps 147:3)

Dissipate the ache further by writing down your feelings every day in a diary.

Then fill your free time with enjoyable activities to avoid thinking about the person you broke up with. Read, watch movies, listen to music, learn French or how to play the guitar.

If you find yourself wallowing in self-pity, avoid being by yourself and take part in group activities such as playing basketball or singing in a choir and you will begin enjoying life again.

LIFE & DEATH

Abortion

Suicide

Death

Death of a Loved One

Sickness

Disability

LIFE & DEATH

ABORTION

Abortion is murder because you are killing a person even though they have not yet been born. So do not abort for God says **You shall not murder.** (Ex 20:13)

Even if no one knows or can see that you are pregnant, God can see your unborn baby in the womb for the psalmist says, **My frame was not hidden from You, when I was made in secret, and skillfully wrought in the lowest parts of the earth. Your eyes saw my substance, being yet unformed. And in Your book they all were written, the days fashioned for me, when as yet there were none of them.** (Ps 139:15-16)

Therefore, do not kill your unborn baby for God has already allotted them days and a purpose for He said to Jeremiah, **Before I formed you in the womb I knew you; Before you were born I sanctified you; I ordained you a prophet to the nations.** (Jer 1:5)

If on the other hand you have already had an abortion, confess your sin to God for **If we confess our sins, He is faithful and just to forgive us our sins and to cleanse us from all unrighteousness.** (1 John 1:9)

Confess and then receive His forgiveness. Forgive yourself, do not engage in premarital sex again and do not live in condemnation for the rest of your life.

LIFE & DEATH:

SUICIDE

When thoughts of killing yourself cross your mind, know that they are from the devil for **The thief does not come except to steal, and to kill, and to destroy.** (John 10:10) So don't entertain the devil or suicidal thoughts in your mind.

Even if your problems are so bad that death seems to be the only way out, do not kill yourself. Learn from Joseph who did not commit suicide even when there seemed to be no end to his problems for his brothers had thrown him into a pit and then sold him into slavery at the age of 17 years. He was then thrown into prison on false charges of attempting to rape his master's wife. Yet, he did not end his life even if there seemed to be no end to his problems.

Even if you have suffered for many years, emulate Joseph who persevered for 13 years from his enslavement to his appointment as Pharaoh's Deputy. If he had committed suicide, he would not have lived to see the beautiful end that God had prepared for him.

So, never commit suicide no matter how dark your today is, for only God knows how bright your tomorrow or your next 10 years will be.

Even if no human being can help you out of your stressful situation like Joseph, instead of contemplating suicide or wondering **From whence comes my help?** (Ps 121:1) remind yourself that **My help comes from the Lord, who made heaven and earth.** (Ps 121:2) for that is where Joseph's help came from for God made Pharaoh dream a dream that only Joseph could interpret. Then ask God to help you.

You can pray, **You have seen, for You observe trouble and grief, to repay it by Your hand. The helpless commits himself to You; You are the helper of the fatherless.** (Ps 10:14)

Then look for help to solve your problems and to deal with the suicidal thoughts. You can talk to your parents, a Pastor or counselor. See chapter on Abuse in the Family.

After that, wait on God to do what only He can do as you meditate on these Scriptures:

● The things which are impossible with men are possible with God. (Luke 18:27)

● All things work together for good to those who love God, to those who are called according to His purpose (Rom 8:28) just as they did for Joseph.

LIFE & DEATH:

DEATH

If your life is threatened by people or diseases pray, for To God the Lord belong escapes from death. (Ps 68:20)

We can see this when King Nebuchadnezzar ordered Killing the wise men; and they sought Daniel and his companions, to kill them (Dan 2:13) because they could not tell him his dream and interpret it. Daniel went to his house, and ... his companions, that they might seek mercies from the God of heaven concerning this secret, so that Daniel and his companions might not perish. (Dan 2:17-18) They prayed and The secret was revealed to Daniel. (Dan 2:19) and their lives were spared.

So pray regardless of what is threatening your life. You can pray, They take counsel together against me, they scheme to take away my life. But as for me, I trust in You, O Lord; I say, "You are my God." My times are in Your hand; deliver me from the hand of my enemies, and from those who persecute me. (Ps 31:13-15)

Then do what you can to protect your life from premature death. Eat healthily, stay out of trouble and respect your parents for God says **Honor your father and your mother, that your days may be long** (Ex 20:12)

Entrust what you cannot do for yourself to God and meditate on Scriptures like this one instead of dwelling on thoughts of dying:

✝ **I shall not die, but live, and declare the works of the Lord.** (Ps 118:17)

LIFE & DEATH:

DEATH OF A LOVED ONE

If someone you love has died, pray, mourn and accept their death as irreversible like David did when his son died and he said, **I shall go to him but he shall not return to me.** (2 Sam 12:23)

If you are being mistreated because your loved ones have died or there are unresolved issues around their death entrust your life to God. Pray hard and work hard to ensure you succeed in life and take care of yourself and your siblings.

If your loved one died from an avoidable cause such as driving while drunk, or not wearing a seat belt, or from a preventable disease like AIDS, learn from it and don't engage in anything that might bring you a sad, similar fate.

LIFE & DEATH:

SICKNESS

If you are sick, pray for yourself to the Lord God **Who heals all your diseases** (Ps 103:3).

You can pray, **Heal me, O Lord, and I shall be healed** (Jer 17:14)

Do not be like King Asa who **Became diseased in his feet, and his malady was severe; yet in his disease he did not seek the Lord, but the physicians. So Asa ... died.** (2 Chr 16:12-13)

Consult medical doctors and consult God for even if your disease is medically incurable and has been termed terminal, God can terminate it and prolong your life as He did for Hezekiah.

Hezekiah was sick and near death ... Then Hezekiah ... prayed to the Lord. (Is 38:1-2) God's reply was, **I have**

heard your prayer, I have seen your tears; surely I will add to your days fifteen years. (Is 38:5)

So, **Pray without ceasing** (1 Thess 5:17) and as you believe that **With God all things are possible** (Matt 19:26) for even studies have shown that prayer works and having faith can speed recovery from illnesses and addictions.

Ask a Pastor to pray for you also for

Is anyone among you sick? Let him call for the elders of the church, and let them pray over him ... And the prayer of faith will save the sick, and the Lord will raise him up. (James 5:14-15)

In addition, live right, take your medications faithfully, eat a balanced diet rich in fruits and vegetables. Avoid processed foods with artificial colors and preservatives. Abstain from alcohol, nicotine and other intoxicants and exercise regularly.

Don't despair for **We do not lose heart. Even though the outward man is perishing, yet the inward man is being** renewed day by day. (2 Cor 4:16) Meditate on these Scriptures to renew your inner self:

🚑 "I will restore health to you and heal you of your wounds," says the Lord. (Jer 30:17)

🚑 Jesus Healed all who were sick (Matt 8:16)

🚑 I shall be made well. (Matt 9:21)

LIFE & DEATH:

DISABILITY

If you have a blind eye, mute tongue, deaf ear, paralyzed limb or another body part that looks or functions differently from most people, don't waste time pitying yourself or feeling inadequate like Moses who **Said to the Lord, "O my Lord, I am not eloquent ... but I am slow of speech and slow of tongue."**

So the Lord said to him, "Who has made man's mouth? Or who makes the mute, the deaf, the seeing, or the blind? Have not I, the Lord?

Now therefore, go, and I will be with your mouth and teach you what you should say." (Ex 4:10-12)

Live your life confidently because God made you, He loves you, He is with you and He will use you mightily if you trust Him to guide you and do for you what you are not able to do for yourself.

Do not focus on your disability even if people constantly talk about it. Focus instead on your education for the brain is great leveler of society. Study and you will own all you want if you believe that **I can do all things through Christ who strengthens me.** (Phil 4:13)

In addition, avoid people who try to make you feel inferior with their words or looks. When they hurt your feelings, cry out to God for He says, "**Vengeance is Mine, I will repay,**" (Rom 12:19)

MONEY

Being Broke / Not Having Money

Lack of School Fees

MONEY:

BEING BROKE/ NOT HAVING MONEY

If you need money, pray to **The Lord your God, for it is He who gives you power to get wealth.** (Deut 8:18)

You can pray, *I pray that I may prosper in all things and be in health, just as my soul prospers.* (ADP 3 John 1:2)

After praying, begin working for wanting to have money won't give you money. Your wishing has to be combined with working for **The soul of a lazy man desires, and has nothing; but the soul of the diligent shall be made rich.** (Prov 13:4) So begin working by making something that you can sell using your talents.

Learn from the parable that Jesus taught of a noble man who was going on a journey and **So he called ten of his servants, delivered to them ten minas, and said to them, "Do business till I come."** (Luke 19:13)

When he returned, he asked those servants **Whom he had given the money, to be called to him, that he might know how much every man had gained by trading.**

Then came the first, saying, "Master, your mina has earned ten minas." And he said to him, "Well done ... because you were faithful in very little, have authority over ten cities," (Luke 19:15-17)

Recognize that God has given each one of us at least one talent and He expects us to use it to "Do business". So use yours to generate some income.

If you can sketch, draw birthday or Xmas cards.

If you can sew, make skirts, shirts or scarves.

If you can sing, start singing in your church choir, birthdays and funerals.

Begin using your talent today. Don't wait to be given an opportunity. Give yourself the chance to succeed for **A man's gift makes room for him, and brings him before great men.** (Prov 18:16)

As you utilize it, know that it isn't really yours for when the servants were accounting for theirs, they said, **"Master, your mina has....."** (Luke 19:16) It is God's talent for He deposited it in you. You may have developed it, but you did not give yourself the ability to sing or sculpt.

So use your gift to glorify God by producing products and services that do not harm others for **Every tree that does not bear good fruit is cut down and thrown into the fire.** (Matt 7:19)

Do not adopt unethical, illegal or immoral practices for **Wealth gained by dishonesty will be diminished, but he who gathers by labor will increase.** (Prov 13:11)

Rise up early. **Do not love sleep, lest you come to poverty; open your eyes, and you will be satisfied with bread.** (Prov 20:13) If tempted to oversleep, remember that **A little sleep, a little slumber, a little folding of the hands to rest; so shall your poverty come like a prowler, and your need like an armed man.** (Prov 24:33-34)

Do not waste your free time playing and joking for **In all** labour there is profit, but idle chatter leads only to poverty. (Prov 14:23)

Follow through your actions to your desired end and do not waste your efforts with silly mistakes or slothfulness for **The lazy man does not roast what he took in hunting, but diligence is man's precious possession.** (Prov 12:27) The lazy hunter sleeps before roasting his meat and in the morning it is not fit for sale or consumption.

Do not let excuses keep your products away from your customers for **The lazy man says, "There is a lion outside! I shall be slain in the streets!"** (Prov 22:13). Be determined and sell them whether it is raining or shining for **The lazy man will not plow because of winter; he will beg during harvest and have nothing.** (Prov 20:4)

Understand also that if you faithfully use your one talent, God will bless you with ten sources of income from it just as He gave the faithful servant **Authority over ten cities** (Luke 19:17).

E.g. if you faithfully use your 1 singing talent, God can bless you with 10 revenue sources:

1. Singing in crusades, concerts, conferences

2. Royalties from radio stations and other companies that play your music

3. Royalties from the use of your music as mobile phone ring tones

4. Your own shop or distribution company that sells your CDs and those of other musicians

5. Your own recording company that charges other musicians to produce their songs

6. Your own music school that teaches how to play musical instruments and gives vocal lessons

7. Teaching music in universities, colleges and schools or tutoring private students

8. Being a consultant to upcoming musicians by critiquing their demo tapes and training them on marketing their music

9. Adjudicating in singing competitions

10. Endorsing products like drinks and soaps

Therefore, do not be like the lazy servant who did not use

his talent and said, **Master, here is your mina, which I have kept put away in a handkerchief** (Luke 19:20) for his talent was taken away from him and you will loose yours if you do not use it.

As you begin to make money, tithe by taking 10% of your income to your local Church and God will protect your business and make it productive for He says **Will a man rob God?**

Yet you have robbed Me!

But you say, "In what way have we robbed You?"

In tithes and offerings. ...

Bring all the tithes into the storehouse, that there may be food in My house, and try Me now in this," says the Lord of hosts, "If I will not open for you the windows of heaven and pour out for you such blessing that there will not be room enough to receive it. And I will rebuke the devourer for your sakes, so that he will not destroy the fruit of your ground, nor shall the vine fail to bear fruit for you in the field." **says the Lord of hosts.** (Mal 3:8-11)

If possible, reinvest 10% of your earnings. E.g. save 10% of your income until you have enough money to buy a tool or a musical instrument or to record your songs in a studio.

Do not also forget the less fortunate for **He who has pity on the poor lends to the Lord, and He will pay back what he has given.** (Prov 19:17)

As you do all this, know you will encounter problems but keep moving forward believing that **He who trusts in the Lord will be prospered.** (Prov 28:25)

Learn from Isaac who encountered problems but never gave up for **Isaac's servants dug in the valley, and found there a well of running water ... But the herdsmen of Gerar quarreled with Isaac's herdsmen, saying, "The water is ours." ... Then they dug another well, and they quarreled over that one also ... And he moved from there and dug another well, and they did not quarrel over it.** (Gen 26:19-22) So persist until you succeed as you meditate on:

$$ **Let the Lord be magnified, who has pleasure in the prosperity of His servant.** (Ps 35:27)

$$He brings out those who are bound into prosperity. (Ps 68:6)

$$Be strong and do not let your hands be weak, for your work shall be rewarded! (2 Chr 15:7)

MONEY:

LACK OF SCHOOL FEES

The Employment Act 2007 allows children aged between 13 and 16 years to be employed in light work that does not endanger their health or interfere with their schoolwork.

You can therefore get a job if you need to pay your school fees or to support yourself and your siblings. Ask your learning institution if you can work for them to pay your fees. Suggest kitchen duties like peeling potatoes and washing dishes or fieldwork like cutting grass or any other job that they would have paid someone to do.

If your institution does not offer that option, ask anyone else who you think can employ you. Do not be shy or proud. Ask one and all for you never know who might be touched by your plight and decide to pay your fees. A good place to begin is in the Church and other Missionary institutions for they may even offer you a scholarship or link you up with sponsors.

As you seek a job or scholarship, know that you have to develop your character so that people can recommend you to reputable institutions and influential persons without hesitation. We see that when King Saul said to his servants, "Provide me now a man who can play well, and bring him to me."

Then one of his servants answered and said, "Look, I have seen a son of Jesse the Bethlehemite, who is skillful in playing, a mighty man of valor, a man of war, prudent in his speech, and a handsome person; and the Lord is with him. (1 Sam 16:17-18)

So do the following to improve your odds of getting a job or scholarship:

$$ Perfect your skills and talents for David was **Skillful in playing** the harp.

$$ Pray, praise God and do good like David for they saw and said **The Lord is with him.**

$$ Don't gossip or lie so you can be trusted like David who was **Prudent in his speech.**

$$ Be well groomed like David who was seen as **A handsome person** and not a smelly shepherd.

$$ Be self confident like David who didn't allow an inferiority complex stop him from playing his harp for the King when he had just been playing it for sheep for he was **A mighty man of valor.**

$$ Don't fear challenges, take the bull by the horns like David, **A man of war** who delivered his sheep from the mouths of lions and bears.

When you do get the scholarship or the job, however menial it may be, **Whatever you do, do it heartily, as to the Lord and not to men, knowing that from the Lord you will receive the reward ... for you serve the Lord Christ. (Col 3:23-24)**

If you cannot get a job, then create one by using your talents to generate an income. Sell cards you have drawn or vegetables you have grown. See chapter on Being Broke / Not Having Money.

Finally, if despite your best efforts you cannot raise your fees, understand that you may have to postpone your education to later in your life. Get a job, study, save, and register for your national exams as a private candidate.

You can also sign up for weekend and evening lessons in a college of your choice.

PARENTS

Obeying Parents

Pressure from Parents

Parents not Trusting You

Parents not Understanding You

Parents Fighting

PARENTS:

OBEYING PARENTS

Children, obey your parents (Eph 6:1)

Hear the instruction of your father, and do not forsake the law of your mother. (Prov 1:8)

Don't be foolish and disobey them for **A fool despises his father's instruction** (Prov 15:5)

Apply your heart to instruction, and your ears to words of knowledge. (Prov 23:12) Let their wise words flow in through your ears and store them in your heart from where you will retrieve them later for you are to **Listen to counsel and receive instruction, that you may be wise in your latter days.** (Prov 19:20)

In addition, you have to respect your parents/ guardians even when they make mistakes for we see that Ham was cursed for being disrespectful while his 2 brothers were blessed because they treated their father Noah respectfully when he was drunk and Became uncovered in his tent. And Ham, the father of Canaan, saw the nakedness of his father, and told his two brothers outside.

But Shem and Japheth took a garment, laid it on both their shoulders, and went backward and covered the nakedness of their father. Their faces were turned away, and they did not see their father's nakedness.

So Noah awoke from his wine, and knew what his younger son had done to him. Then he said: "Cursed be Canaan; a servant of servants he shall be to his brethren. (Gen 9:21-25)

Finally, whenever you are tempted to disobey or disrespect your parents/guardians, remind yourself that:

- Honor your father and your mother, that your days may be long upon the land (Ex 20:12)

- The eye that mocks his father, and scorns obedience to his mother, the ravens of the valley will pick it out, and the young eagles will eat it. (Prov 30:17)

- The way of a fool is right in his own eyes, but he who heeds counsel is wise. (Prov 12:15)

PARENTS:
PRESSURE FROM PARENTS

Your parents/guardians pressurize you to study because they want you to excel academically and in life. Even if you plan to pursue a career in music, theatre or sports you still need an education in order to manage your money well.

So don't get irritated as they want the best for you and it is for your own good for **If you are wise, you are wise for yourself, and if you scoff, you will bear it alone.** (Prov 9:12)

Accept also, that what you think are unrealistic expectations from your parents/guardians may not be as their knowledge and experiences enable them to see your untapped potential and what you need to do to exploit it.

Therefore if your parents/guardians or teachers say that you can get an A in chemistry even though you have been getting C's, believe them, believe that you can get an A and study aiming for that A.

Finally, understand that parents/guardians exert positive pressure on their children when they are at home so that they can resist negative pressure once they leave the house for the Bible tells them to **Train up a child in the way he should go, and when he is old he will not depart from it.** (Prov 22:6) So humbly succumb to their pressure for they press you to mould you into a success.

PARENTS:

PARENTS NOT TRUSTING YOU

Sometimes parents/guardians act like they do not trust teenagers because they understand what it means to be a teenager and they don't want you to blunder because of your hormones. They therefore restrain you with their rules until when they deem that you can restrain yourself.

Parents/guardians also know that a single mistake lasting 10 minutes can negatively affect the next 30 years of your life. E.g. a single act of premarital sex can mar the rest of your life with an incurable disease, a single injection of an illicit drug can enslave you for the rest of your life and a single accident while you are drunk can paralyze you for the rest of your life.

Since no loving parent/guardian wants such dire long term consequences after a few minutes of folly for their child, they protect you by preventing you from being in such situations. So do not misinterpret their caution as mistrust.

Your parents/guardians have also invested heavily in the tangibles of education, clothing and food into your life. For this reason, they do not want you or anyone else to mess with their precious investment i.e. You.

They want you to mature into a responsible, productive adult with your own home, job and family even if they will already have died. Thus, they supervise your development and decline your requests to go to places they think may harm their investment.

You parents/guardians have also heavily invested the intangibles of love and care into your life (even if you did not feel it).

Therefore, do not misconstrue their love for you as mistrust for if your parent/guardian did not love you, they wouldn't care if you went out and got AIDS, syphilis and herpes. If they did not care about you, they would not care who your friends were and what you did with them for it would not matter to them if you ended up a drug addicted criminal or a homeless alcoholic.

Therefore, understand that just as our Heavenly Father gave us the 10 commandments for our own good, your earthly father and mother and guardians lay down their rules with your best interests at your heart.

Understand also that God does not prohibit stealing or lying to deny us the pleasure we would get from those activities. He does so to protect us from their harmful repercussions.

Similarly, your parents/guardians do not stop you from going to parties and other places to prevent you from enjoying life. They do so to protect you from the dangers lurking there.

As your parents/guardians can see all the things that can potentially go wrong in those situations, even if you did not plan for them to go wrong, they deny you the permission to go to those events to spare you the pain of finding out for yourself.

Therefore, since you do not rebel against God's

commandments but you try your best to obey them, do not defy your parents'/guardians' rules and regulations. Obey them without question even if you don't understand the rationale behind them.

If on the other hand, you have done something that made your parents/guardians not trust you, work at regaining their trust again.

Do things that demonstrate to them that you are trustworthy. E.g. work very hard in school and bring the best possible grades home. Engage in constructive extra-curricular activities and let them see the awards or cash you generate from them. Be responsible in the house by doing your chores without being reminded twice every day. Use your initiative and take up other responsibilities like washing dishes or taking care of your younger siblings to demonstrate your maturity.

Be responsible and demonstrate that you can be trusted and once they see that you have a stable head on your shoulders, they will give you more leeway.

In addition, do not complain and compare your parents/guardians with those of your friends who allow them to do things or wear clothes that your parents/guardians will not allow. Throwing tantrums while claiming that they do not trust you only shows them that you do not deserve to be trusted and they will feel more justified to keep a tighter rein on you until you "grow up".

Finally, do not hide your friends. Parents/ guardians know the extreme pressure that peers can exert on you and even if they trust you, they may not trust your secret friends. As they stand to loose a lot, they will not give you permission to go out with people they don't know. So bring your friends home and spend time studying, listening to music or watching movies, so that your parents/guardians can see them, and see that they are good, decent young people who will not influence you adversely.

PARENTS:

PARENTS NOT UNDERSTANDING YOU

If you feel that your parents/guardians do not understand you, try to understand their point of view so that you can help them appreciate yours.

Put yourself in their position as parents/guardians trying to bring up a good child in this day and age to figure out their logic. As you do so, remember that they may have been brought up with different rules and that their decisions usually arise from a caring heart. For these reasons, give them the benefit of doubt.

To help you understand them better, picture a curious 3 year old pulling a tablecloth oblivious to the sharp knife lying on it. You forbid him and he throws a tantrum because he does not understand why you are limiting his fun for he can't see the knife from his vantage point. The child thinks it is just an innocent game of pulling the tablecloth and thinks you don't understand that children need to play. However, you can see the knife and the danger it poses to him so you punish him if he persists in pulling it despite your warnings for you would rather see him crying from a smack on his wrist than from a bleeding facial laceration.

Therefore, respect your parents'/guardians' judgment even if you think they don't understand you. Trust that one day when you have your own teenagers, you will understand their viewpoint just as the 3 year old would comprehend why he was being denied the chance to pull a tablecloth if he suddenly grew taller and saw the razor-sharp knife perched on the table.

PARENTS:

PARENTS FIGHTING

If your parents/guardians fight frequently, pray asking God to intervene in their relationship and help them resolve their conflicts in a better way.

You can pray, **What God has joined together, let not man separate.** (Matt 19:6) Neither let money or misfortune separate them.

When they begin fighting, leave the room so that you do not hear their slurs, slaps or screams. Pray and ask God to protect you and your brothers and sisters so that their fights do not leave emotional scars in your lives.

If you are unable to get out of earshot, pray from right where you are.

If your parents/guardians separate or divorce, focus on God and your future and not on the painful family situation.

If one of your parents/guardians leaves with some of your siblings, mentally unburden yourself by forwarding your family to God in prayer, **Casting all you care upon Him, for He cares for you.** (1 Pet 5: 7) Ask Him to heal all the physical, emotional, social and financial wounds of your family.

Then talk to a trusted adult or counselor and live the rest of your life to the best of your ability without blaming yourself even if you were mentioned in their pre-breakup fights.

RELIGION

The Lord God Almighty

Jesus Christ God's Son

The Holy Spirit

Feeling You Lack Faith

Living Right

RELIGION:

THE LORD GOD ALMIGHTY

The fool has said in his heart, "There is no God" (Ps 14:1) Don't be a fool. Believe there is one true God and read your Bible to know Him.

Jesus taught that God, our Heavenly Father loves us like the father of the youth who asked for his inheritance, **Journeyed to a far country, and there wasted** all his money on riotous living.

Then **There arose a severe famine in that land, and he began to be in want.** He got a job feeding pigs **And he would gladly have filled his stomach with the pods that the swine ate, and no one gave him anything.** However, he realized he didn't have to live like a pig in grime so **He arose and came to his father.**

But when he was still a great way off, his father saw him and had compassion, and ran and fell on his neck and kissed him.

And the son said to him, "Father, I have sinned against heaven and in your sight, and am no longer worthy to be called your son."

But the father said to his servants, "Bring out the best robe and put it on him, and put a ring on his hand and sandals on his feet. And bring the fatted calf here and kill it, and let us eat and be merry; for this my son was dead and is alive again; he was lost, and is found. And they began to be merry. (Luke 15:11-24)

Likewise, if you decide to stop living an immoral illicit life, He'll forgive you for He is **God, ready to pardon, gracious and merciful, slow to anger, abundant in kindness.** (Neh 9:17)

He will receive you even if you are still a long way from being the perfect teen once you stop wallowing in sin and come to Him for the prodigal son was still a great way off, he was still covered with filth and smelling like a pig when his father saw him, embraced and welcomed him home.

So ask for His forgiveness today and He will forgive you, receive you and there will be a great feast in heaven for Jesus said, **I say to you that likewise there will be more joy in heaven over one sinner who repents than over ninety nine just persons who need no repentance.** (Luke 15: 7)

After repenting don't return to the sinful pigsty life and in so doing behave like **"A dog returns to his own vomit,"** and, **"a sow, having washed, to her wallowing in the mire."** (2 Pet 2:22)

RELIGION:

JESUS CHRIST GOD'S SON

The Father loves the Son, and has given all things into His hand. He who believes in the Son has everlasting life; and he who does not believe the Son shall not see life, but the wrath of God abides on him. (John 3:35-36)

Believe in Jesus and open your heart's door to Him for He says: **Behold, I stand at the door and knock. If anyone hears My voice and opens the door, I will come in to him.** (Rev 3:20)

Let Him into your life today by deciding to live righteously and then **You confess with your mouth the Lord Jesus and believe in your heart that God has raised Him from the dead, you will be saved.** (Rom 10:9)

Open your mouth right now and say, "Jesus Christ is the Son of God" and believe in your heart that He died on the cross for your sins and rose from the dead. Do this and you will be saved from eternal condemnation and you will have everlasting life after you die **For there is no other name under heaven given among men by which we must be saved.** (Acts 4:12)

Read 1 chapter of your Bible everyday so that you can know what He would like you to do and then don't sin intentionally for **Let everyone who names the name of Christ depart from iniquity.** (2 Tim 2:19)

Then develop a personal relationship with Him by talking to Him everyday in prayer. Ask Him for what you need and thank Him for what you receive. Let Him help you in all your problems for Jesus also came to:

To preach the gospel to the poor - He will teach you the Good News whether you are spiritually poor or physically poor

To heal the brokenhearted - He will mend your heart whether broken by people or problems.

To proclaim liberty to the captives - He will free you from alcohol, cigarettes, drugs, immorality, phobias or whatever has bound you.

And recovery of sight to the blind - He will restore your inner vision or outer sight.

To set at liberty those who are oppressed - He will liberate you from abusive situations.

To comfort all who mourn - He will console you when you grieve.

To give them beauty for ashes, the oil of joy for mourning, the garment of praise for the spirit of heaviness (Luke 4:18 & Is 61:1-3) He will replace the damaged things in your life with beautiful ones, the sadness with joy, and the depression with cheerfulness.

RELIGION:

THE HOLY SPIRIT

The Holy Spirit assists us for Jesus said, **It is to your advantage that I go away; for if I do not go away, the Helper will not come to you; but if I depart, I will send Him to you.** (John 16:7)

He helps us pray for **The Spirit also helps in our weaknesses. For we do not know what we should pray for as we ought, but the Spirit Himself makes intercession for us** (Rom 8:26)

He also directs us for as Jesus said, **When He, the Spirit of truth, has come, He will guide you in all truth.** (John 16:13) So pray to be filled with the Holy Spirit for **Your heavenly Father give the Holy Spirit to those who ask Him** (Luke 11:13)

RELIGION:

FEELING YOU LACK FAITH

What is faith?

Faith is the substance of things hoped for, the evidence of things not seen. (Heb 11:1)

To have faith therefore, is to believe that you'll receive the things that you hope to receive and to see those things with your mind's eye even if you can't see them with your physical eyes.

Don't think that you don't have any faith for **God has dealt to each one a measure of faith.** (Rom 12:3)

Increase your measure of faith by listening to the Word of God for **Faith comes by hearing, and hearing by the word of God** (Rom 10:17)

If doubts enter your mind after listening to God's Word being preached or reading your Bible, chose to believe God's Word and you will have increased your faith.

If the doubts are strong pray and say, **Lord, I believe; help my unbelief!** (Mark 9: 24)

In addition, strengthen your measure of faith by using it. Pray for something small and believe that you'll get it because once you do, your faith will have been strengthened and it will be easier to believe God for bigger things.

Finally, know that even with "weak" or "little" faith you can achieve a lot for Jesus said, **If you have faith as a mustard seed, you can say to this mulberry tree, 'Be pulled up by the roots and be planted in the sea,' and it would obey you.** (Luke 17:6)

RELIGION:

LIVING RIGHT

Live righteously and do the right thing for **The eyes of the Lord are on the righteous, and His ears are open to their prayers; But the face of the Lord is against those who do evil.** (1 Pet 3:12)

To pray for help, you can say, **Cleanse me from secret faults. Keep back your servant also from presumptuous sins; let them not have dominion over me. Then I shall be blameless, and I shall be innocent of great transgressions.** (Ps 19:12-13)

Then read your Bible everyday for **All Scripture is given by inspiration of God, and is profitable for doctrine, for reproof, for correction, for instruction in righteousness.** (2 Tim 3:16)

These instructions in righteousness include:

1 I am the Lord your God … you shall have no other gods before Me.

2 You shall not make for yourself a carved image … you shall not bow down to them

3 You shall not take the name of the Lord your God in vain

4 Remember the Sabbath day to keep it holy

5 Honor your father and your mother

6 You shall not murder.

7 You shall not commit adultery.

8 You shall not steal.

9 You shall not bear false witness

10 You shall not covet your neighbor's house … wife … nor anything that is your neighbor's. (Ex 20)

The Bible also helps you differentiate the right thing to do from what feels right as they may not be the same thing for **There is a way that seems right to a man, but its end is**

the way of death. (Prov 14:12)

E.g. It may feel right to engage in premarital sex but at its end is death by AIDS.

Be like Daniel, who as a youth decided that he would live righteously. While undergoing his training, **Daniel purposed in his heart that he would not defile himself**(Dan 1:8) and he refused to eat food and drink wine that would do so.

Likewise, you must also resolve that you will live right and not defile yourself whether it is sexually, or with drugs, alcohol or junk food because **Your body is the temple of the Holy Spirit who is in you, whom you have from God** (1 Cor 6:19)

Ignore those who mock you for God says, **Listen to Me, you who know righteousness, you people in whose heart is My law: do not fear the reproach of men, nor be afraid of their insults. For the moth will eat them up like a garment, and the worm will eat them like wool;** (Is 51:7-8)

Then meditate on Scriptures like these to stay on the right path:

✝ No good thing will He withhold from those who walk uprightly. (Ps 84:11)

✝ The salvation of the righteous is from the Lord; He is their strength in the time of trouble. (Ps 37:39)

✝ The Lord will not allow the righteous soul to famish (Prov 10:3)

SCHOOL

Bullying

Prefects

Obeying Teachers

Teachers Abusing Students

Preparing for Exams

Poor Academic Performance

SCHOOL:

BULLYING

If you are being harassed by prefects or bullied by other students by being insulted, beaten, kicked, threatened, stripped naked, having your books, food and money stolen or any other method, pray and ask God to help you.

You can pray, **Plead my cause, O Lord, with those who strive with me; Fight against those who fight against me. Take hold of shield and buckler, and stand up for my help.** (Ps 35:1-2)

After praying, inform the school's administration about the bullying and how the prefects are abusing their power. You can inform them verbally or by writing a letter to a teacher or a member of the school's Board of Governors. Your letter should contain 100% truthful details of the specific incidences with the names of the prefects and bullies involved.

E.g. On 4th March 2012 after night prep Prefect Joe and Bob beat up Ken behind dorm A and took his pocket money of Ksh 100.

Your letter can remain anonymous if you fear repercussions from the prefects or bullies should they discover you have been reporting them.

After you have done what you can about your stressful situation, strengthen yourself by meditating on these Scriptures:

🔔 The Lord executes righteousness and justice for all who are oppressed. (Ps 103:6)

🔔 The Lord is on my side. (Ps 118:6)

🔔 I know that the Lord will maintain the cause of the afflicted, and justice for the poor. (Ps 140:12)

Then continue studying hard and praying hard and you will succeed like Nehemiah did even in the middle of many problems if you have **A mind to work.** (Neh 4:6)

If you are not being bullied or harassed by prefects, but other students are suffering from their abuses, pray and ask God to show you how you can help them so that you can all learn in an environment where no one's life, health or academic performance is compromised.

SCHOOL:

PREFECTS

If prefects are harassing you by beating you, "confiscating" your pocket money or any other way, read the chapter on Bullying.

If you are a prefect, do not abuse your power because God is watching for **There is no creature hidden from His sight, but all things are naked and open to the eyes of Him to whom we must give account.** (Heb 4:13)

Be fair for **It is not good to show partiality in judgment. He who says to the wicked, "You are righteous," him the people will curse; nations will abhor him. But those who rebuke the wicked will have delight, and a good blessing will come upon them.** (Prov 24:23-25)

In addition, **Do not withhold good from those to whom it is due, when it is in the power of your hand to do so.** (Prov 3:27)

Then, meditate on these Scriptures so that you can fulfill your responsibilities fairly:

🔔 To turn aside the justice due a man before the face of the Most High, or subvert a man in his cause – the Lord does not approve. (Lam 3:35-36)

🔔 The violence of the wicked will destroy them, because they refuse to do justice. (Prov 21:7)

🔔 It is not good to show partiality to the wicked, or to overthrow the righteous in judgment. (Prov 18:5)

SCHOOL:

OBEYING TEACHERS

When you feel rebellious and you just want to defy your teachers, tame those feelings and obey them even if you do not feel like obeying for **The wise in heart will receive commands, but a prating fool will fall.** (Prov 10:8)

Disobeying teachers will lead to failure in your studies, wasting years of your life suffering from diseases and addictions **And you mourn at last, when your flesh and body are consumed.**

And say: "How I have hated instruction, and my heart despised correction! I have not obeyed the voice of my teachers (Prov 5:11-13)

Therefore **Hear instruction and be wise, and do not disdain it.** (Prov 8:33)

When tempted to disobey your teachers, remind yourself that:

❗ He who is often rebuked, and hardens his neck, will

suddenly be destroyed, and that without remedy. (Prov 29:1)

❗ The way of a fool is right in his own eyes, but he who heeds counsel is wise. (Prov 12:15)

❗ Whoever loves instruction loves knowledge, but he who hates correction is stupid. (Prov 12:1)

SCHOOL:

TEACHERS ABUSING STUDENTS

Male and female teachers can sexually abuse students of both genders.

It can begin subtly with the teacher being friendly and having a ready ear for your woes. This is not bad and you should listen to their advice until their attention crosses the moral line and they start speaking or touching you inappropriately.

Sexual abuse can also begin overtly with the teacher blatantly telling you that if you resist their sexual advances they will punish you by failing you, caning you or myriad other ways.

Regardless of how it begins, aim to stop it and protect yourself from pregnancy, physical and emotional illnesses.

First, pray for guidance and ask God to intervene in your situation. You can pray, **I am afflicted very much; Revive me, O Lord, according to Your word.** (Ps 119:107)

Then tell the teacher to stop harassing you. If you cannot tell them because of their threats or intimidation, let your head teacher know. If you are not comfortable telling them in the face, write them an anonymous letter detailing your situation with 100% honesty.

Do not suffer in silence as you can ask for help from many other people e.g.

Parents & other close relatives

Inform them either verbally or by writing to them.

Pastors

Seek the advice of Pastors or church leaders.

Doctors

Consult them for treatment of physical injuries or diseases and emotional issues like depression.

Lawyers

Consult them for legal advice as it is a criminal offence to abuse a student. See chapter on Helpful Numbers.

The Police

If you need to report the abusers, ensure your statement is 100% truthful.

Your Member of Parliament

Consider writing a letter to your MP or the MP of the area where the school is situated for help. In addition, see chapter on Abuse in the Family.

After you have physically done whatever you can do about your abusive situation, and you are waiting for it to change for the better, surrender it to God by acknowledging that **The battle is not yours, but God's** (2 Chr 20:15)

Give the situation to God but do not give up on it. Continue fighting spiritually with your prayers and praise songs. Believe that He will help you emerge victorious and you will have peace of mind to study successfully even in the middle of the extremely stressful situation.

SCHOOL:

PREPARING FOR EXAMS

To ensure you pass exams, do the following:

📋 Pray and ask God to help you as He helped Daniel and his 3 friends **For these four young men, God gave them knowledge and skill in all literature and wisdom. (Dan 1:17)**

When their schooling was over, Nebuchadnezzar **The king interviewed them, and among them all none was found like Daniel, Hananiah, Mishael, and Azariah** (also known as Belteshazzar, Shadrach, Meshach, and Abed-Nego) **... in all matters of wisdom and understanding about which the king examined them, he found them 10 times better than all** (Dan 1:19-20) the other student.

📋 Do the right thing at the right time even when your parents/guardians, teachers or prefects are not watching you. Do not hunch over your books and pretend to be studying whether you are in a day or boarding school for Daniel and his 3 friends were studying away from their parents yet they excelled.

- Study consistently by setting specific study times and keeping them.

- Summarize the key points of each topic from your class notes and textbooks in a revision exercise book each weekend while the lessons are still fresh in your mind as this will reduce your revision time when the exams draw near.

E.g. In mathematics, write down the formulas for each topic with one example of how to apply it.

- Begin revising early in order to cover all topics before you sit for the exams.

- Test yourself by doing past tests or revision papers in the time allocated for the real exam. Mark them and read the topics you got wrong.

◻ Keep your study area clean and clutter-free to reduce time wastage and confusion. Open the windows daily to let in fresh air as decreased oxygen levels may cause reduced concentration and fatigue. Improve the lighting to avoid eyestrain and headaches. Sit with your back straight to reduce backaches and other pains.

◻ Take 15 minutes breaks after studying for

1-2 hours to rest and replenish your energy. You can take a walk, chat, eat, or drink water.

◻ Manage your time well to ensure you have a time to study ... a time to sleep ... a time to eat ... **A time to laugh ... a time to keep silence** (Eccl 3) Wake up early to study instead of tossing in your bed for **As a door turns on its hinges, so does the lazy man on his bed.** (Prov 26: 14)

◻ Eat healthily and do not pollute your body with junk food, alcohol and drugs like Daniel who **Purposed in his heart that he would not defile himself with the portion of the king's delicacies, nor with the wine which he drank.** (Dan 1:8)

☐ Exercise regularly to help you relax, clear your mind and reduce stress by playing the games are played in your school.

☐ Sleep for 7 - 9 hours each night to rest your body and avoid sleep depravation which results in poor concentration and low retention.

☐ Do not be distracted by students who are not serious with their studies. Do not break rules that may result in suspension from your classes. Ignore those who try to discourage you or make you afraid of exams. Keep a positive mental attitude and you will do much better than if you let thoughts of failure flood your mind.

☐ Do your best for **Daniel distinguished himself ... because an excellent spirit was in him.** (Dan 6:3) Pay utmost attention in class to recall easier. Do your homework and study hard to the best of your ability. Then **Commit your works to the Lord, and your thoughts will be established.** (Prov 16:3)

SCHOOL:

POOR ACADEMIC PERFORMANCE

If you did not get the marks you wanted in your exams, analyze why you did not do well. Is it because you did not study enough or pay attention in class or do you need extra tutoring?

Once you have identified the reason, change it. Do more revision tests. Pay attention in class. Ask questions for clarification. Request extra coaching. See chapter on Preparing for Exams.

Then be determined to do better in the next exams. If you have to repeat the exams or school year, then so be it. Repeat it knowing that since you have experience, you will do better the second or third time round.

Don't entertain discouraging thoughts as they will weaken your resolve to excel and restrain you from working hard. When the discouraging thoughts come into your mind as you study, remind yourself that **With God all things are possible.** (Mark 10: 27)

If your relatives or friends mock you because you failed, remind yourself of Mic 7:8 which says, **Do not rejoice over me, my enemy; when I fall, I will arise; when I sit in darkness, the Lord will be a light to me.**

If after you have done your best and your conscience is clear before God that you did your utmost best yet you still failed your exams, do not let your results stress you. Release them to God and ask Him what you should do with the rest of your life.

SEX

Fighting Temptation

Fornication

Masturbation

Pornography

Homosexuality & Lesbianism

Sugar Daddies & Sweet Mommies

Stopping Sexual Sin

Teenage pregnancy

Rape

SEX:

FIGHTING TEMPTATION

Whenever you are tempted, remind yourself that **No temptation has overtaken you except such as is common to man; but God is faithful, who will not allow you to be tempted beyond what you are able, but with the temptation will also make the way of escape, that you may be able to bear it.** (1 Cor 10:13)

This means that you are not the only one facing that type of temptation. Other teenagers in your community, country and continent are also facing the same temptation and they are overcoming it because God will never allow you to face a temptation that you can't resist for with each temptation there is always a way out.

Therefore when tempted, look for a way out of the tempting situation and leave with haste like Joseph did when Potiphar' wife **Caught him by his garment, saying, "Lie with me." But he left his garment in her hand, and fled and ran outside** (Gen 39:12) without wasting time asking for his garment.

Do the same and do not look back or come back.

Do not think that you can stay and outsmart your tempters who represent the devil for he is **The tempter** (1 Thess 3:5)

As you look for your exit, know that Jesus can help you for **We do not have a High Priest who cannot sympathize with our weaknesses, but was in all points tempted as we are, yet without sin. Let us therefore come boldly to the throne of grace, that we may obtain mercy and find grace to help in time of need.** (Heb 4:15-16)

Pray asking Jesus to strengthen you and show you how to exit the situation, if it isn't obvious!

Do not listen to your tempter's smooth words and grand promises for **With her enticing speech she caused him to yield, with her flattering lips she seduced him. Immediately he went after her, as an ox goes to the slaughter ... he did not know that it would cost his life.** (Prov 7: 21-23)

Do not debate with your tempters why you will not sin. Emulate Jesus and quote the Bible if you have to speak to them. The devil tempted Him thrice and each time He answered saying

"**It is written...**" (Matt 4) and quoted Scriptures.

He did not answer:

"I don't FEEL like doing it" or

"I don't WANT to do it" or

"I don't THINK it's a good idea" or

"I KNOW that is wrong".

He begun and ended his conversation with the tempter by quoting the Word of God and that is what you also must do.

Simply quote Scriptures to them and end the conversation. You can say:

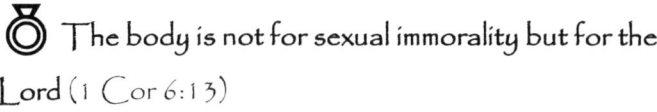 The body is not for sexual immorality but for the Lord (1 Cor 6:13)

🔔 Present your bodies a living sacrifice, holy, acceptable to God, which is your reasonable service. (Rom 12:1)

🔔 Do not be overcome by evil, but overcome evil with good. (Rom 12:21)

SEX:

FORNICATION

Do not be deceived. Neither fornicators, nor idolaters, nor adulterers, nor homosexuals, nor sodomites, nor thieves, nor covetous, nor drunkards, nor revilers, nor extortioners will inherit the kingdom of God. (1 Cor 6:9-11)

To break free from engaging in premarital sex, remember the mnemonic **STOP**

S Set a date to stop.

T Think about why you want to stop fornicating and write down your reasons. Carry the paper for quick reference when tempted.

O Omit people and places that encourage you to fornicate from your diary.

Ask yourself:

 Who do I fornicate with?

Then stop spending time with that person or those people for you are **Not to keep company with sexually immoral people** (1 Cor 5:9)

If you know someone fornicates, **Do not go near the door of her house, lest you give your honor to others, And your years to the cruel one; Lest aliens be filled with your wealth, And your labors go to the house of a foreigner;** (Prov 5:8-10)

Stay away from fornicators for you will spoil your reputation and suffer for many years with sexually transmitted infections as you enrich drug manufacturers by buying their medications.

 Where do I fornicate?

○ Is it in your home?

If so, do not allow the people you used to fornicate with into your home.

- Is it in their homes or dorms?

If so, do not visit them.

- Is it in secret rendezvous?

If so, skip them. Do not go to meetings or dates in secluded places.

- Is it in discos, bars, boarding and lodgings?

If so, stay away from places where people fornicate freely for **A man who wanders from the way of understanding will rest in the assembly of the dead.** (Prov 21:16)

⚑ Put obstacles between you and fornicating by asking yourself:

⊙ Why do I fornicate?

⊙ Is it because you are attracted to a specific person?

If so, avoid them or relate to them only in group settings and in public places.

⊙ Is it because of peer pressure?

If so, stay away from those peers even if you have to be alone.

See chapters on Negative Peer Pressure, Positive Peer Pressure, Love and Lust.

⊙ When do I fornicate?

⊙ Is it during school holidays, weekends or in the evenings after school?

Then spend your free time and extra energy in positive extra-curricular activities like playing badminton or the bass guitar.

⊙ Is it after watching certain movies or reading some books or magazines?

If so, don't watch or read them. Get rid of them.

⊙ Is it after drinking alcohol?

Then stop drinking it for alcohol makes one feel less inhibited thus more likely to fornicate. **Be sober, be vigilant; because your adversary the devil walks about like a roaring lion, seeking whom he may devour. Resist him** (1 Pet 5:8-9)

SEX:

MASTURBATION

Masturbation or pleasuring yourself sexually, can become addictive. The guilt and shame you may feel after masturbating can lower your self-confidence and adversely affect your relationships with the opposite sex.

To break free from masturbation, remember the mnemonic **STOP**

S Set a date to stop.

T Think about why you want to stop masturbating. Write down your reasons. Carry the paper with you all the time. Refer to it when tempted.

O Omit people and places that encourage you to masturbate from your diary. Ask yourself:

♂♀ Who do I masturbate with?

♂♀ Is it when you are alone?

If so, find other things to do during that time.

♂♀ Is it in the presence of other people?

If so, avoid them and those who extol it.

♂♀ Where do I masturbate?

♂♀ Is it in your bathroom or bedroom?

If so, restrict your time in those rooms. Go to the bathroom only to clean or relieve yourself. Use your bedroom only to sleep or read.

♂♀ Is it in places or rooms you can avoid?

If so, stay away from them.

P Put obstacles between you and masturbating by asking yourself:

♂♀ Why do I masturbate?

♂♀ Is it because of peer pressure?

If so, choose to be alone rather than with those peers. See chapters on Negative Peer Pressure and Positive Peer Pressure.

♂♀ When do I masturbate?

♂♀ Is it in the evenings after school?

If so, spend your free time engaged in positive activities like playing football or the flute.

♂♀ Is it after watching certain movies or reading some novels?

If so, get rid of all books, magazine, videos and DVDs that entice you to have sex even if it is with yourself.

♂♀ Is it after drinking alcohol?

If so, stop imbibing.

♂♀ Is it when you are feeling lonely or stressed?

If so, find other ways of dealing with those emotions such as listening to relaxing music and reading. See chapter on Loneliness.

♂♀ Is it when you are idle?

If so, cure your boredom by using your hands constructively to develop your talents e.g. by drawing, weaving or baking.

♂♀ Is it when you cannot sleep at night?

If so, exercise during the day, take a warm shower and read a good book in bed such as your Bible to soothe your mind so that you can fall asleep.

SEX:
PORNOGRAPHY

Pornography (porn) begins as "harmlessly" looking at sexually explicit images in books, magazines, movies or websites.

It rapidly grows into a very addictive habit as the graphic images grab you, control your life and adversely affect your relationships with God and the opposite sex.

Pornography is not harmless for Jesus said **Whoever looks at a woman to lust for her has already committed adultery with her in his heart.** (Matt 5:28) Therefore, if you are lustfully gazing at sexual images, you are committing adultery.

To break free from surfing or watching or reading pornographic material, remember the mnemonic STOP:

S Set a date to stop.

T Think about why you want to stop looking at pornographic images and write down your reasons. Carry the paper with you all the time and look at it when you are tempted to do so.

O Omit people and places that encourage you to watch pornography from your diary.

Ask yourself:

📼🖱 Who do I watch pornography with?

📼🖱 Is it when you are alone?

If so, decide that **I will set nothing wicked before my eyes.** (Ps 101:3) and find other things to do during that time.

📼🖱 Is it with your friends?

If so, stop spending time with them.

📼🖱️ Where do I watch pornography?

📼🖱️ Is it in your home?

If so, only buy or borrow decent family movies.

📼🖱️ Is it in other people's homes?

If so, don't visit them.

📼🖱️ Is it in video libraries or shops?

If so, stay away from them.

Put obstacles between you and watching pornography by asking yourself:

Why do I watch pornography?

Is it because of peer pressure?

If so, avoid those peers. See chapter on Negative Peer Pressure.

Is it because it is available?

If so, get rid of all pornographic material in your possession and install pornographic website blockers in your computer. Do so for it is easier to get rid of the pornographic material than get to rid of your eyes which are making you sin for Jesus said, **If your right eye causes you to sin, pluck it out and cast it from you; for it is more profitable for you that one of your members perish, than for your whole body to be cast into hell.** (Matt 5:29)

When do I watch pornography?

Is it during school holidays, weekends or in the evenings after school?

If so, spend your free time and extra energy in positive extra-curricular activities like playing rugby or the recorder.

📼❦ Is it after drinking alcohol or using drugs?

If so, don't use the addictive substances.

📼❦ Is it when you are feeling lonely?

If so, see chapter on Loneliness.

📼❦ Is it when you cannot fall asleep at night?

If so, exercise during the day so that you can be physically exhausted and read your Bible in bed to calm your mind so that you can sleep.

SEX:

HOMOSEXUALITY & LESBIANISM

Do not be deceived. Neither fornicators, nor idolaters, nor adulterers, nor homosexuals, nor sodomites, nor thieves, nor covetous, nor drunkards, nor revilers, nor extortioners will inherit the kingdom of God. (1 Cor 6:9-11)

The Word of God is clear that homosexuality and lesbianism are repugnant to Him for He says **You shall not lie with a male as with a woman. It is an abomination.** (Lev 18:22)

To break free from homosexuality or lesbianism, remember the mnemonic STOP

S Set a date to stop.

T Think about why you want to stop engaging in homosexuality or lesbianism and write down your reasons. Carry the paper with you all the time to refer to it when you are tempted to do so.

O Omit people and places that encourage you to engage in homosexuality or lesbianism from your diary. Ask yourself:

♂♀ Who do I engage in homosexuality or lesbianism with?

Then stop spending time with those people, avoid those who justify it and do not listen to their arguments. See chapter on Negative Peer Pressure.

♂♀ Where do I engage in homosexuality or lesbianism?

♂♀ Is it in your home?

If so, do not allow the people you used to engage in homosexuality or lesbianism with into your home.

♂♀ Is it in their homes or dorms?

If so, don't visit them or take their calls.

♂♀ Is it in secluded places, "special" parties, "exclusive" events, discos or bars?

If so, steer clear of them. Stay on the straight and narrow straight path and **Do not enter the path of the wicked, and do not walk in the way of evil. Avoid it, do not travel on it; Turn away from it and pass on.** (Prov 4:14-15)

♂ Put obstacles between you and engaging in homosexuality or lesbianism by asking yourself:

♂♀ Why do I engage in homosexuality or lesbianism?

♂♀ Is it because you feel attracted to a specific person?

If so, avoid them or relate to them only in group settings and in public places.

♂♀ Is it because of peer pressure?

If so, see chapter on Negative Peer Pressure and read your Bible everyday for **When wisdom enters you heart ... discretion will preserve you; understanding will keep you, to deliver you from the way of evil ... from those who leave the paths of uprightness to walk in the ways of darkness ... and delight in the perversity of the wicked** (Prov 2:10-14)

♂♀ When do I engage in homosexuality or lesbianism?

♂♀ Is it during school holidays, weekends or after school in the evenings?

If so, spend your free time and extra energy in positive extra-curricular activities like playing tennis or the trumpet.

♂♀ Is it after watching certain videos or reading some magazines?

If so, get rid of the ones you own and do not buy or borrow others.

♂♀ Is it after drinking alcohol or using drugs?

If so, drink non-alcoholic beverages and do not use any other addictive substances.

SEX:

SUGAR DADDIES & SWEET MOMMIES

The works of the flesh are evident, which are: adultery, fornication, uncleanness, lewdness ... those who practice such things will not inherit the kingdom of God. (Gal 5:19-21)

Learn from Joseph and avoid relationships with sweet mommies or sugar daddies for **His master's wife cast longing eyes on Joseph, and she said, "Lie with me." But he refused and said ... How then can I do this great wickedness, and sin against God?** (Gen 39:7-9)

Joseph resisted this sugar mommy because God says **You shall not commit adultery** (Ex 20:14) and you should do the same.

Fear the Lord and depart from evil. It will be health to your flesh, and strength to your bones. (Prov 3:7-8) Depart from the sugar daddies or sweet mommies and you will be departing from AIDS, gonorrhea, chlamydia, cervical cancer and getting pregnant.

Another reason to avoid relationships with sugar daddies or sweet mommies is that usually you are just a toy to them. They may profess to love you but when they get tired of playing with you, they will go out and buy themselves another toy just as they have bought you by buying you meals, clothes or giving your pocket money.

Since they almost always have the upper hand in the relationship, they will also play with your emotions to manipulate you to do things you may not be willing to do.

In addition, your parents and society in general may not approve of your relationship and you may have to conduct it secretly and in fear.

To break free from having relationships with sugar daddies or sweet mommies, remember the mnemonic STOP:

S Set a date to stop.

T Think about why you want to stop having relationships with sugar daddies or sweet mommies and write down your reasons. Carry the paper with you all the time and refer to it when you are tempted to be involved with one.

O Omit people and places that encourage you to have relationships with sugar daddies and sweet mommies from your diary. Ask yourself:

💍 Who are the sugar daddies or sweet mommies that I relate with?

Then avoid that person or those people.

💍 Where do I meet and greet the sugar daddies or sweet mommies?

💍 Is it through introductions from your peers?

If so, avoid those peers who enjoy and advocate relationships with sugar daddies or sweet mommies. See chapter on Negative Peer Pressure.

- Is it in nightspots and other carousing places? If so, stop going to those places.

- Is it at school?

If so, see chapter on Teachers Abusing Students.

- Is it in offices or shops?

If so, avoid their business premises and homes.

- Is it on the road or bus stops?

If so, stop talking to strangers or accepting lifts from them or consenting to free rides from public service vehicles.

- Is it over the internet?

If so, avoid sites where adults prey on teenagers and children.

P Put obstacles between you and the sugar daddies or sweet mommies. Ask yourself:

○ Why do I have relationships with sugar daddies or sweet mommies?

○ Is it because of peer pressure?

If so, see chapter on Negative Peer Pressure.

○ Is it because you are attracted to people of that age group?

If so, seek counseling to find out why you prefer dates of your parents' age group.

○ Is it because you need the money?

If so, see chapter on Being Broke/Having No Money.

○ Is it because they pay your school fees?

If so, see the chapter on Lack of School Fees.

⭕ When do I have relationships with sugar daddies or sweet mommies?

⭕ Is it in the evenings after school or during school holidays?

If so, spend your time and youthful energy on positive extra-curricular activities like generating money with your talents or playing chess or the clarinet.

⭕ Is it when you are feeling lonely?

If so, see chapter on Loneliness.

SEX:

STOPPING SEXUAL SIN

Flee sexual immorality.

Every sin that a man does is outside the body, but he who commits sexual immorality sins against his own body. (1 Cor 6:18)

Do you not know that your bodies are members of Christ?

Shall I then take the members of Christ and make them members of a harlot?

Certainly not!

Or do you not know that he who is joined to a harlot is one body with her?

For "the two," He says, "shall become one flesh."

But he who is joined to the Lord is one spirit with Him. (1 Cor 6:15-17)

Therefore do not let sin reign in your mortal body, that you should obey it in its lusts.

And do not present your members as instruments of unrighteousness to sin, but present yourselves to God (Rom 6:12-13)

For this is the will of God, your sanctification:

that you should abstain from sexual immorality;

that each of you should know how to posses his own vessel in sanctification and honor,

not in passion of lust …

That no one should take advantage of and defraud his brother in this matter, because the Lord is the avenger of all such (1 Thess 4:3-6)

To stop fornicating, masturbating, watching pornography, engaging in homosexuality or lesbianism and having relationships with sugar daddies or sweet mommies do the following;

💍 📷 🖱 ♂ ♀ Get saved (see chapter on Jesus Christ) and commit yourself **Now to Him who is able to keep you from stumbling** (Jude 24) Pray every day for strength to overcome temptation and break the habit.

💍 📷 🖱 ♂ ♀ Join a Bible teaching Church, ask your Pastor to pray for you and attend deliverance services.

💍 📷 🖱 ♂ ♀ Consult a Christian counselor, doctor or psychologist to help you resolve the deeper issues like emotional pain and low self esteem that may be leading you to sin.

💍 📷 🖱 ♂ ♀ Remind yourself of the consequences of sexual sin e.g.

💍 ♂ ♀ Contracting HIV and developing tuberculosis, candidiasis, Kaposi's sarcoma, lymphomas, meningitis, chronic diarrhea, herpes zoster, toxoplasmosis, brain abscesses and blindness

💍 ♂ ♀ Contracting herpes simplex

⚭♂♀ Contracting hepatitis B

⚭♂♀ Contracting syphilis

⚭♂♀ Contracting vaginosis

⚭♂♀ Contracting trichomoniasis

⚭♂♀ Contracting chlamydia

⚭♂♀ Contracting chancroid

⚭♂♀ Contracting gonorrhea

⚭♂♀ Contracting scabies

⚭♂♀ Developing cancer of the cervix

⚭♂♀ Developing cancer of the vagina

⚭♂♀ Developing cancer of the vulva

♂♀ Developing cancer of the penis

♂♀ Developing cancer of the anus

⚭♂♀ Developing genital warts

♂♀ Developing anal warts

⚭♂♀ Becoming infested with pubic lice

⚭ Getting pregnant or impregnating someone

⚭♂♀ Life imprisonment for having sex with a child

(defilement) of less than 11 years or for 20 years or more for defiling a 12-15 year old.

💍 Interrupting your education to give birth and work to support the baby.

💍 Missing normal teenage years as you take on the responsibilities of a teenage parent.

💍📼🖱♂♀ Hurting your parents

💍📼🖱♂♀ Getting a bad reputation

💍♂♀ Being unable to get babies when you are older and want them.

💍 📼 🖱 ♂ ♀ **Keep your heart with all diligence, for out of it spring the issues of life.** (Prov 4:23) Do not put dirty thoughts in your heart and mind by watching movies, TV programs or surfing sites with sexually explicit images as they will stimulate you to sin sexually. Watch family movies or educational programs.

Don't put dirty thoughts in your heart and mind by listening to secular music that invokes sexual vibes or exalts fornication. Listen to Christian praise and worship music as it will positively modify the mood in your mind and room.

Don't put dirty thoughts in your heart and mind by reading sexually explicit books or magazines as they feed your imagination with fantasies and strengthen the desire to fornicate. Read the Bible, schoolbooks and motivational books.

💍 📷 🖱 ♂ ♀ Be patient and persistent in your effort to stop sinning sexually. If you slip and start re-sinning, ask God to forgive you, analyze why you slipped by going through the 4 steps of **STOP**, forgive yourself and then stop once again.

In addition, **Put off, concerning your former conduct, the old man which grows corrupt according to the deceitful lusts, and be renewed in the spirit of your mind** (Eph 4:22-24)

💍 📷 🖱 ♂ ♀ **Be renewed in the spirit of your mind** (Eph 4:23) by replacing all thoughts that encourage you to fornicate, masturbate, watch pornography, engage in homosexuality or lesbianism and have relationships with sugar daddies or sweet mammies with Scriptures so that you can and start thinking in a different way.

💍 📷 🖱 ♂♀ Read 1 chapter of the Bible everyday to learn the Scriptures you'll use to renew your mind, replace the unrighteous thoughts and help you fight the temptation to sin sexually. E.g.:

💍 📷 🖱 ♂♀ The body is not for sexual immorality but for the Lord, and the Lord for the body. (1 Cor 6:13)

💍 📷 🖱 ♂♀ Flee sexual immorality. (1 Cor 6:18)

💍 📷 🖱 ♂♀ Abstain from fleshly lusts which war against the soul. (1 Pet 2:11)

Save these Scriptures in your mind like the Psalmist who said **You word I have hidden in my heart that I might not sin against you.** (Ps 119:11)

SEX:

TEENAGE PREGNANCY

If you get pregnant, pray for courage to tell your parents/guardians. It is better to tell them than for them to discover and they will discover for they can see the changes going on in your body even if you can't see them or feel them.

Pray and read your Bible daily. Go to Church and speak to a Pastor. If you are shunned, watch TV services or listen to them on radio.

Don't abort for God says **You shall not murder.** (Ex 20:13) Pray for strength to carry the pregnancy to term. After delivery, if you do not want the baby, give them up for adoption. There are women who have longed for a baby for years and they will lovingly take care of yours.

SEX:

RAPE

Regardless of whether you are male or female, if you have been raped or forced to have sex, go to a hospital immediately to be examined and given medications to prevent getting HIV, other sexually transmitted infections and pregnancy.

Ask to be referred to a counselor to receive psychological help for the feelings of shame, guilt, filth, worthlessness, despair and depression which may engulf you.

Pray everyday asking God to heal you mentally, physically and emotionally so that you can regain your self esteem, forgive the rapists and forget the incident so that it doesn't mar your future relationships.

Read your Bible everyday and repeat these Scriptures to yourself to help you recover:

♥ There is hope in your future, says the Lord. (Jer 31:17)

♥ Fear not, for I am with you; Be not dismayed, for I am your God. I will strengthen you, Yes, I will help you, I will uphold you with my righteous right hand. (Is 41:10)

♥ You are my hiding place and my shield; I hope in Your word ... Uphold me according to Your word, that I may live; and do not let me be ashamed of my hope. (Ps 119:114-116)

SOCIETY

Celebrities

Fashion

Crime

Corruption

Cultural Practices

Global Warming & Pollution

SOCIETY:

CELEBRITIES

Do not compare yourself with the air brushed, computer generated images of famous people in magazines as you will be frustrating yourself.

This is because these stars usually spend a lot of money and time with the best make up artists, hairdressers, designers and stylists preparing for those photo shoots so that they can look that amazing in the magazines.

Many of them also spend hard cash and hours with plastic surgeons, cosmetic dermatologists, personal trainers and follow restrictive diets to develop and maintain their looks because their livelihood depends on it.

These measures, which make them look like stars, may not be affordable or practical for someone leading a regular life, so do not torment yourself by trying to look like a celebrity.

Do not also idealize the frames of famous persons in TV programs, movies or music videos and starve yourself to be like them. Eat healthily, exercise regularly and thank God for your body regardless of whether you are petite or plus size because you are **Wonderfully made**. (Ps 139:14)

Develop your talents so that you can shine and be a star in some area of your life e.g. you can be the science star or the sprinting star or the soloist star or the soccer star of your class.

SOCIETY:

FASHION

Clothes communicate. Choose those that convey the right message about you and resist pressure from peers, TV programs, movies and magazines to dress in a certain way.

Appreciate other people's style but develop your own by experimenting with outfits that are not tight or revealing

Do not cross dress for **A woman shall not wear anything that pertains to a man, nor shall a man put on a woman's garment, for all who do so are an abomination to the Lord.** (Deut 22:5)

To create your signature style wear clothes that suit your body type and hide your flaws.

⚘ If you want to appear slimmer wear black or dark colours like navy blue.

- If you want to appear taller wear clothes with vertical designs.

- If you want to appear bigger wear white or brightly colored clothes in roomy designs like flared skirts or trousers.

- If you want to appear shorter wear clothes with horizontal designs.

- If you have a big tummy avoid brightly colored belts and pleated skirts or trousers.

- If you have knock-knees or bow legs wear flowing skirts or baggy trousers.

N.B. These are rules of cloth and not of stone so you can break them and still look trendy.

To build your wardrobe, buy one new or second hand blouse or shirt in a material, color and design that you really like. The next time you get money, buy a black or dark blue trouser or skirt. Then buy black shoes to complete your outfit.

Continue building wardrobe by buying one chic piece of clothing at a time always ensuring that it matches with what you have at home. In this way, your wardrobe will be color coordinated, you will always look good and like you have many outfits when in fact you are just mixing and matching the few, fabulous pieces of clothing that you have.

However, **Do not let your adornment be merely outward – arranging the hair, wearing gold, or putting on fine apparel – rather let it be the hidden person of the heart with the incorruptible beauty of a gentle and quiet spirit, which is very precious in the sight of God.** (1 Pet 3:3-4)

So as you beautify your outward appearance, beautify your inner person for God because **Man looks at the outward appearance, but the Lord looks at the heart.** (1 Sam 16:7)

Therefore, each morning give yourself this Spiritual Facial for your heart.

- Cleanse it by confessing your sins

- Tone it by thanking God for your blessings

- Steam it with forgiveness to open up and let go of bitterness and vengeance

- Apply the mask of salvation to remove sins

- Spot treat the blemishes of worry and doubt with faith and trusting God.

- Moisturize it with prayer to keep it radiant, supple and healthy

Then **Be clothed with humility.** (1 Pet 5:5) and the **Fragrance of His knowledge** (2 Cor 2:14)

SOCIETY:

CRIME

If you have been engaging in criminal activities, remember the mnemonic **STOP** to break free from them.

S Set a date to stop.

T Think about why you want to stop engaging in criminal activities and write down your reasons. Carry the paper with you all the time and refer to it when you are tempted to do so.

O Omit people and places that encourage you to commit crimes from your itinerary. Ask yourself:

🚓 Who do I engage in criminal activities with?

Then stop spending time with those people for **Whoever is a partner with a thief hates his own life** (Prov 29:24) When they approach you, say, **Depart from me, you evil doers, for I will keep the commandments of my God!** (Ps 119:115)

If you do so by yourself, engage in legal activities during the hours you used to commit the crimes.

🚓 Where do I engage in the criminal activities?

🚓 Is it in other peoples' homes, dorms, isolated places, crowded places or carousing places?

If so, stay away from those places.

🚓 Is it in a place that you cannot avoid such as the local shop?

If so, only go there when you have a constructive agenda e.g. to buy milk.

Put obstacles between you and the criminal activities by asking yourself:

🚔 Why do I engage in criminal activities?

🚔 Is it because you are pressured to be delinquent?

If so, avoid the villains and hang out with virtuous pals or by yourself. If they persistently pester you, remind yourself that **Folly is joy to him who is destitute of discernment, but a man of understanding walks uprightly.** (Prov 15:21) See chapter on Negative Peer Pressure.

Even if they are making lots of money from their criminal activities don't be jealous of them now for you won't envy them when they are being punished in this world and in the next. **Do not ... be envious of the wicked; for there will be no prospect for the evil man; the lamp of the wicked will be put out.** (Prov 24:19-20)

🚔 Is it because you need money?

If so, see chapter on Being Broke / Not Having Money and remember that **Wealth gained by dishonesty will be diminished, but he who gathers by labor will increase.** (Prov 13:11).

🚓 Is it because you break the law just for the sake of flouting it?

If so, know that you should obey the law as you **Submit yourselves to every ordinance of man for the Lord's sake, whether to the king as supreme, or to governors, as to those who are sent by him for the punishment of evildoers and for the praise of those who do good for this is the will of God** (1 Pet 2:13-14)

🚓 Is it because you break the law "just for fun"? If so, remember that **To do evil is like sport to a fool, but a man of understanding has wisdom.** (Prov 10:23) So be wise and have legal fun.

🚨 When do I engage in criminal activities?

🚓 Is it during school holidays, weekends or in the evenings after school?

If so, spend your free time and extra energy in positive extra-curricular activities like playing hockey or the violin.

🚔 Is it when you are bored?

If so, know that **The way of life winds upward for the wise, that he may turn away from hell below.** (Prov 15:24) So don't be stupid and break the law as you will trigger a downward spiral of your life from punishment by parents, teachers, law enforcers, diseases and hell. So, whether it is your neighbour in class, the dorm or in the estate, **Let none of you think evil in your heart against your neighbour; and do not love a false oath. For all these are things that I hate, says the Lord.** (Zech 8:17)

🚔 Is it after watching certain DVD's or reading some paperbacks?

If so, get rid of all them and read those that espouse positive virtues.

🚔 Is it after drinking alcohol or using drugs?

If so, don't use addictive substances for some like alcohol lower your inhibition and make you do things you wouldn't do when not under their influence. Their intense cravings may also compel you to commit crimes to buy the drugs.

🚓 Is it when you want to be popular your peers?

If so, decide to seek popularity with God by living right rather than seek popularity with peers. See chapter on Negative Peer Pressure.

🚓 Is it when you are feeling lonely?

If so, see chapter on Loneliness.

Other things you can do to stop committing crimes include:

🚓 Get saved (see chapter on Jesus Christ). **Pray that you may not enter into temptation.** (Luke 22:40)

🚓 Join a Bible teaching Church and ask your Pastor to pray for you. Attend deliverance services and the prayers and testimonies of other Christians will strengthen you.

🚓 Consult a Christian counselor or doctor to help you deal with issues like kleptomania that may be contributing to your criminal activities.

🚔 Be very determined to stop committing crimes. If you restart, analyze why you did by going through the 4 steps of STOP, forgive yourself and then stop again.

🚔 Read 1 chapter of your Bible everyday to learn the Scriptures you will use to remove the illegal thoughts from your mind and help you fight the temptation to engage in criminal activities. E.g.:

🚔 As righteousness leads to life, so he who pursues evil pursues it to his own death. (Prov 11:19)

🚔 Getting treasures by a lying tongue is the fleeting fantasy of those who seek death. (Prov 21:6)

🚔 A man with an evil eye hastens after riches, and does not consider that poverty will come upon him. (Prov 28:22)

If you do not engage in crime, but live in a crime infested area, pray to God for protection and trust Him. **Do not be afraid of sudden terror, nor of trouble from the wicked when it comes; for the Lord will be your confidence, and will keep your foot from being caught.** (Prov 3:25-26)

Do not endanger your life by being nosy or going out at night. For peace of mind, meditate on Scriptures such as these when you have to:

🚓 I will deliver you from the hand of the wicked, and I will redeem you from the grip of the terrible. (Jer 15:21)

🚓 Though I walk through the valley of the shadow of death, I will fear no evil, for You are with me (Ps 23:4)

🚓 He shall give His angels charge over you, to keep you in all your ways. (Ps 91:11)

SOCIETY:

CORRUPTION

The fool has said in his heart, "There is no God." They are corrupt. (Ps 14:1)

Do not dupe yourself that anyone gets away with corruption for **Woe to those who seek deep to hide their counsel far from the Lord, and their works are in the dark; they say, "Who sees us?" and "Who knows us?"** (Is 29:15) because God is watching us and He will punish even those who are not punished by the law here on earth.

Begin your fight against corruption by deciding that you will never be corrupt.

Then pray for it to end. Know that one upright person praying fervently can change a country through prayer for **The effective, fervent prayer of a righteous man avails much. Elijah was a man with a nature like ours, and he prayed earnestly that it would not rain; and it did not rain on the land for 3 years and 6 months. And he prayed again, and the heaven gave rain, and the earth produced its fruit. (James 5:16-18)

If you see those who have enriched themselves corruptly living in mansions and driving luxury vehicles, **Do not envy the oppressor, and chose none of his ways; for the perverse person is an abomination to the Lord.** (Prov 3:31-32)

If you are suffering unjustly due to corruption copy Jesus who **Leaving us an example, that you should follow His steps ... When He suffered, He did not threaten, but committed Himself to Him who judges righteously.** (1 Pet 2:21-23)

Commit your case to God and depend on Him for justice as you meditate on these Scriptures:

🚓 He who walks righteously and speaks uprightly;

he who despises the gain of oppressions,

who gestures with his hands, refusing bribes,

who stops his ears from hearing of bloodshed, and shuts his eyes from seeing evil:

He will dwell on high; his place of defense will be the fortress of rocks, bread will be given him, his water will be sure. (Is 33:15-16)

🚔 You shall take no bribe, for a bribe blinds the discerning and perverts the words of the righteous. (Ex 23:8)

🚔 One who increases his possessions by usury and extortion gathers it for him who will pity the poor. (Prov 28:8)

SOCIETY:
CULTURAL PRACTICES

If your culture's customs are stressing you, know that the law protects you from some of them e.g. marrying someone younger than 16 years old is an offence with a jail term and fine. Thus, you can seek help, see chapter on Helpful Numbers.

If you can't do anything about the rites you are being forced to undergo, work hard to become an influential person and change the laws that permit those practices or offer alternative solutions to protect other teenagers.

In addition, do not speak negatively of other cultures and tribes for **He who is devoid of wisdom despises his neighbor, but a man of understanding holds his peace.** (Prov 11:12)

SOCIETY:

GLOBAL WARMING & POLLUTION

When you see in the news or read in the papers or feel the harsh effects of climatic changes, use your God given authority to preserve the environment for He said, **Let them have dominion over the fish of the sea, over the birds of the air, and over the cattle, over all the earth and over every creeping thing that creeps on the earth.** (Gen 1:26)

Conserve water by harvesting rainwater and closing or reporting all dripping taps. Switch off lights in empty rooms to save electricity. Use recycled papers and plastics. Make a cloth bag that you can use multiple times to carry things instead of using plastic paper bags.

If your environment is germ or vermin infested and has been polluted with non-degradable plastics and scrap metal, organize a clean up day. If your neighbors don't cooperate, pick up the litter yourself and put up notices reminding them not to litter.

If the litter or polluted air and water is adversely affecting your health, know that you have a right to a clean environment and you can go to court to defend that right. Understand also that the environmental law in Kenya law prohibits causing excessive noise that disturbs others.

If you can't stop those polluting your environment, work hard to leave the area. It may take years, but you will not feel trapped in the dirt because you will be doing something constructive to get out of it.

YOU

Puberty

Body Shape & Self Image

Comparison Syndrome

Who am I?

Gender Realization

Why am I here?

Negative Thoughts

Negative Words

Your Past

Your Future

YOU:

PUBERTY

Puberty is the period when a boy or girl starts to mature sexually. These changes, which begin at around 12 years in boys and 10 years in girls, are triggered by hormones and take several years.

Enlargement of the testicles & penis, hair growth in the face, armpits & pubic area and deepening of the voice are signs of puberty in boys.

Breast development, hair growth in the armpits & pubic area and beginning menstruation are signs of puberty in girls. In addition, both girls and boys have rapid weight and height increases.

Learn to accept these changes as they are part of your normal growth and development.

YOU:

BODY SHAPE & SELF IMAGE

As your body changes from that of a boy or girl to that of a man or woman, you may feel uncomfortable with the new form that it is taking.

This may be because you may have gained a lot of weight. Or you may have developed acne. Or your hands, legs, feet, ears or nose may seem to be growing at a faster rate than the rest of your body and thus appear disproportionately larger.

To avoid this discomfort from destroying your self confidence, accept the changes and stand in front of a mirror and affirm yourself saying:

☻ Father God, **Your hands have made me and fashioned me** (Ps 119:73) and **I am fearfully and wonderfully made.** (Ps 139:14)

Say it as you wash your face in the morning, as you brush your teeth in the evening, and every time you catch a glimpse of yourself in a mirror.

Believe that you are a wonderful person who is wonderfully made whether or not you resemble Mr. or Miss Universe for the Bible says so.

If someone teases you or looks at you badly, ignore them and say to yourself:

😊 Father God, **Your hands have made me and fashioned me** (Ps 119:73) and **I am fearfully and wonderfully made.** (Ps 139:14)

In addition, change what you can change about your appearance.

E.g. Seek treatment for acne, eat healthily and exercise regularly to manage your weight.

What you cannot change, give to God in prayer and focus on excelling in life.

E.g. Commit your big nose and ears to God and commit your mind to excelling in your studies.

When you begin excelling, you will find that compliments will begin to replace insults. Your self esteem will also rise and the teasing will hurt you less and less.

E.g. If you have a very big head and begin excelling in maths, you will be respected for your mathematical ability and not teased as much for your big head. In addition, you will begin to love your big head since it holds a big, bright brain.

If you are taller and scrawnier than your peers and focus on excelling in basketball, you will find that applause will replace mockery as your scoring ability improves and they admire your performances in the court.

Your self confidence will also increase as you begin to see your body shape as an asset and you won't care if you are teased about it.

So, do not spend the whole day in front of a mirror lamenting about your body or feeling sorry for yourself. Spend the day improving yourself and thinking about yourself positively, the way God wants you to see yourself.

Change the way your think about yourself and don't waste your time waiting for your enemies to change the way they think or talk about you. They may not change and even if they do, they may not let you know as it serves their purposes to keep you feeling insecure.

YOU:

COMPARISON SYNDROME

Do not envy and compare yourself with anyone because **Envy is rottenness to the bones. (Prov 14:30)** It poisons you with bitterness, confusion and self-contempt for **Where envy and self-seeking exist, confusion and every evil thing are there. (James 3:16)**

Do not cast longing eyes on others while disdaining yourself for **You shall not covet your neighbor's house; you shall not covet your neighbor's wife, nor his male servant, not his female servant, nor his ox, nor his donkey, nor anything that is your neighbor's. (Ex 20:17)**

Do not envy your classmate because of their classic physique, chic clothes, charming personality, commendable grades, competence on the tennis court, countless friends, caring parents, cool cousins, copious pocket money, cutting edge mobile phone or anything else that is theirs.

If you admire something that someone else has, work to get your own or improve what you have.

E.g. If your neighbor in class scores 100% in mathematics, don't envy and hate them. Study to score your highest possible mark. If it is 50%, work hard to attain 50%. The next term, work harder to score 60%. Thus, you will feel good about your 60% even when others get 100%.

If your buddy is a swift sprinter, don't begrudge them because of their speed. Train consistently and if you do not qualify for the short races, compete in the marathon or walking races.

If one of your friends has a perfect figure don't resent them because of it. Eat healthily and exercise regularly to refine your God given form and you will not be jealous of theirs as you become more satisfied with yours.

If what you admire in another person you cannot develop in yourself e.g. model height or the speed to bolt 100 meters in 10 seconds, then develop and perfect a talent you were born with. See chapter on Body Shape and Body Image.

Therefore, do not waste another second suffering from self-pity as it is self-defeating. Do not spend another day depressing yourself by trying to express yourself as someone else. Improve and perfect the original masterpiece that God made i.e. you. Be the best you that you can be and not the best copy of someone else.

YOU:

WHO AM I?
SEARCH FOR SELF-IDENTITY

If you have been wondering "Who am I?", look to the Bible for your answers. It says:

☻ You are a child of God

I will be a Father to you, and you shall be My sons and daughters, says the Lord Almighty. (2 Cor 6:18)

☻ Jesus is your friend

You are My friends if you do whatever I command you. (John 15:14)

☻ Your are Christ's diplomat here on earth

We are ambassadors for Christ (2 Cor 5:20)

Let the foundation of your self-identity, self-respect, security and significance be that you are God's child, Jesus' friend and ambassador.

Build on your identity by living the way Christ's diplomat should behave and your positively congruent behaviour will reinforce your positive self identity just as steel reinforces concrete.

In addition, choose and emulate a role model who embodies that identity. It can be your Pastor or his wife, or a teacher or a Biblical role model like Daniel or the Proverbs 31 Woman.

Then join a group which supports your positive self identity. This can be a Christian church youth group where you will interact with other like minded teenagers and receive teaching to further bolster your positive self-identity and Christ-like characteristics.

YOU:

GENDER REALIZATION/ GENDER IDENTITY

The Bible gives us perfect examples of how men and women of God should behave. Let these Biblical men and women be your role models.

Young men aspire to be a man who is **Blameless, as a steward of God, not self willed, not quick-tempered, not given to wine, not violent, not greedy for money, but hospitable, a lover of what is good, sober-minded, just, holy, self-controlled, holding fast the faithful word as he has been taught.** (Titus 1:7-9)

Let Daniel and his friends Shadrach, Meshach and Abed-Nego who were these types of men, even from their youth, be your role models for:

♂ Daniel was blameless, just and loved doing good for **Daniel distinguished himself above the governors and satraps, because an excellent spirit was in him; and the king gave thought to setting him over the whole realm. So the** governors and satraps sought to find some charge against Daniel concerning the kingdom; but they could find no charge or fault, because he was faithful; nor was there any error or fault found in him. (Dan 6:3-4)

♂ Daniel was hospitable, not quick-tempered or violent. When the wise men were to die for not knowing the king's dream, **They sought Daniel and his companions, to kill them. Then with counsel and wisdom Daniel answered Arioch, the captain of the king's guard, who had gone out to kill the wise men. Then he Went in and asked the king to give him time.** (Dan 2:13-16)

♂ Daniel was sober-minded and not given to wine for **Daniel purposed in his heart that he would not defile himself with the portion of the king's delicacies, nor with the wine** (Dan 1:8) He asked to be exempted from ingesting them.

♂ Daniel was self-controlled and not self-willed for he often fasted. He says **I ate no pleasant food, no meat or wine came into my mouth** (Dan 10:3) for three weeks.

♂ Daniel was not greedy for money. When the king promised him a gold chain for decoding the writing on the wall, he said **Give your rewards to another; yet I will read the writing to the king, and make known to him the interpretation.** (Dan 5:17)

♂ Daniel was holy and held fast to prayer even when facing death. When a law forbidding prayer was passed, **In his upper room, with his windows open toward Jerusalem, he knelt down on his knees three times that day, and prayed and gave thanks before his God, as was his custom since early days.** (Dan 6:10) He was thrown to the lions but God protected him for as he said **I was found innocent before Him; and also, O king, I have done no wrong before you.** (Dan 6:22)

♂ Shadrach, Meshach and Abed-Nego also held fast to their faith even when facing death for they said, **Our God whom we serve is able to deliver us from the burning fiery furnace, and He will deliver us from your hand, O king. But if not, let it be known to you, O king, that we do not serve your gods, nor will we worship the gold image which you have set up.** (Dan 3:17-18)

Young ladies let the Prov 31:10-31 woman be your role model.

♀ Her clothing is fine linen and purple ... Strength and honor are her clothing ...

She cultivates inner and outer beauty by being upright, principled and dressing stylishly.

♀ She opens her mouth with wisdom, and on her tongue is the law of kindness.

She does not hurt others with her wise words.

♀ She extends her hand to the poor

She helps the less fortunate in her society.

♀ She ... willingly works with her hands ... She also rises while it is yet night ... And does not eat the bread of idleness

She is hardworking and gets up early.

♀ She … provides food for her household, and a portion for her maidservants … She is not afraid of snow for her household, for all her household is clothed with scarlet

She provides for her family and workers' needs and is not afraid of tough economic times for she has insured and ensured that her family is secure.

♀ She seeks wool and flax … She makes linen garments and sells them, and supplies sashes for the merchants

She is a manufacturer and wholesale distributor who buys raw materials, makes high quality products and then sells them to the retailers.

♀ She considers a field and buys it; from her profits she plants a vineyard.

She's a smart businesswoman, investing in real estate and reinvesting profits.

YOU:

WHY AM I HERE?
THE PURPOSE OF YOUR LIFE

If you've been wondering, "Why was I created?" or "What is the meaning of my life?" understand that God made you for a specific task (i.e. your Life's Purpose) for **We are His workmanship, created in Christ Jesus for good works, which God prepared beforehand that we should walk in them.** (Eph 2:10)

To discover your Life's Purpose, know that it usually involves using your gifts or talents to serve others.

Our talents differ because we have different Life Purposes and **There are diversities of gifts, but the same Spirit ... And there are diversities of activities, but it is the same God who works all in all.** (1 Cor 12:4-6)

Having then gifts differing according to the grace that is given to us, let us use them: ... he who teaches, in teaching, he who exhorts, in exhortation ... he who leads, with diligence; he who shows mercy with cheerfulness. (Rom 12:6-8)

If you are gifted in teaching, tutor your mates. If you have the gift of encouragement, egg on the disheartened. If you have the gift of leadership, be a just prefect. **If any one speaks, let him speak as the oracles of God.** (1 Pet 4:11) Rap Christian inspirational songs or recite motivational poems.

If you are talented in crafts, use your gift to fulfill your Life's Purpose like Bezalel of whom the Lord said, **I have filled him with the Spirit of God, in wisdom, in understanding, in knowledge, and in all manner or workmanship, to design artistic works, to work in gold, in silver, in bronze, in cutting jewels for setting, in carving wood, and in all manner of workmanship ... that they may make all that I have commanded you.** (Ex 31:3-6)

So, As each one has received a gift, minister it to one another, as good stewards of the manifold grace of God. (1 Peter 4:10)

Use your talents and let the world know for no one **Light a lamp and put it under a basket, but on a lampstand, and it gives light to all who are in the house. Let your light so shine before men, that they may see your good works and glorify your Father in heaven.** (Matt 5:15-16)

If your Life's Purpose isn't clear, pray **That you may be filled with the knowledge of His will in all wisdom and spiritual understanding** (Col 1:9)

Then begin to **Walk worthy of the Lord, fully pleasing Him, being fruitful in every good work** (Col 1:10) at home, in school and at church. Let being an obedient child, a diligent student and faithful Christian be your Life's Purpose now.

As you do so, ask God to show you what else He wants you to do for we learn from Namaan's maid that you are never too young or in too tough circumstances that God can't use you.

Naaman, commander of the army of the king of Syria, was a great and honorable man in the eyes of his master, because by him the Lord had given victory to Syria. He was also a mighty man of valor, but a leper. (2 Kin 5:1)

And the Syrians had gone out on raids, and had brought back captive a young girl from the land of Israel. She waited on Naaman's wife. Then she said to her mistress, "If only my master were with the prophet who is in Samaria! For he would heal him of his leprosy." (2 Kin 5:2-3)

This girl was in a stressful situation as she was a prisoner of war forced to work as a maid in the home of the commander of the army that had abducted her from her country.

However, she didn't stop believing in God for she told her boss about the prophet of God Elisha, Naaman went to him and he was healed of leprosy. She fulfilled her Purpose which may have been to let the Syrian army commander and king know that the true God –who was able to heal leprosy- was the God of Israel and not the ones they worshipped in Syria.

So ask God what you should do for your age will not hinder Him from using you if you live right for **Josiah was 8** years old when he became king, and he reigned 31 years ... And he did what was right in the sight of the Lord (2 Kin 22:1-2)

Don't belittle yourself and give excuses like "**Ah, Lord God! Behold, I cannot speak, for I am a youth.**" (Jer 1:6) For God's reply to Jeremiah was, "**Do not say, 'I am a youth.' For you shall go out to all to whom I sent you, and whatever I command you, you shall speak. Do not be afraid of their faces, for I am with you to deliver you,**" says the Lord. (Jer 1:7-8)

In addition, do not let others belittle you. **Let no one despise your youth, but be an example to the believers in word, in conduct, in love, in spirit, in faith, in purity.** (1 Tim 4:12)

YOU:

NEGATIVE THOUGHTS

Choose your thoughts carefully for your thoughts form your feelings, shape your speech, build your behavior and create your character **For as he thinks in his heart, so is he.** (Prov 23:7)

If you constantly think evil thoughts, you'll make sinful choices, engage in illegal activities and become a crook. If you constantly think godly thoughts, you will make moral choices, engage in legal activities and become a good person.

So protect yourself and do not pollute your mind with negativity from your present stressful situation, past experiences, family, friends, the society or the media.

Negative thoughts can also stress you and depress you even when they are not true. E.g. If you hear a loud noise and you think it is gunfire, you will get stressed even if is not.

So, even if you are in a genuinely stressful situation, do not increase your stress levels by thinking negatively or focusing on the potentially negative outcomes of your situation.

Do not be conformed to this world, but be transformed by the renewing of your mind (Rom 12:2) Do not let your thoughts agree with the negativity of your situation. Instead, rejuvenate your mind by reading the Word of God.

Replace every negative thought in your mind with a positive Scripture so that you can maintain a positive state of mind even in negative stressful situations.

Replace thoughts of failure by thinking that **I can do all things through Christ who strengthens me.** (Phil 4:13)

Replace thoughts of impossibility by thinking that **With men it is impossible, but not with God; for with God all things are possible.** (Mark 10: 27)

Replace thoughts of defeat by thinking that **Thanks be to God who always leads us in triumph in Christ** (2 Cor 2:14)

Replace thoughts of fear by thinking that **The Lord is my helper; I will not fear.** (Heb 13: 6)

Replace thoughts of ugliness by thinking that **I am fearfully and wonderfully made.** (Ps 139:14)

YOU:

NEGATIVE WORDS

Your own words can be your own source of stress for A fool's lips enter into contention, and his mouth calls for blows. A fool's mouth is his destruction, and his lips are the snare of his soul (Prov 18:6-7)

So change your speech to steer clear of stress for He who guards his mouth preserves his life, but he who opens wide his lips shall have destruction. (Prov 13:3)

Moreover, He who would love life and see good days, let him refrain his tongue from evil, and his lips from speaking deceit. (1 Pet 3:10) So regulate your speech for negative words will harm you if spoken but are harmless if swallowed.

To change your words, you have to change your mind for A good man out of the good treasure of his heart brings forth good; and an evil man out of the evil treasure of his heart brings forth evil. For out of the abundance of the heart his mouth speaks. (Luke 6:45)

So change and cleanse your mind in order to change and cleanse your mouth. See chapter on Negative Thoughts.

Every morning pray, Let the words of my mouth and the meditation of my heart be acceptable in Your sight, O Lord, my strength and my Redeemer. (Ps 19:14)

Then decide that you'll be Swift to hear, slow to speak (James 1:19) for Even a fool is counted wise when he holds his peace; When he shuts his lips he is considered perceptive. (Prov 17:28)

Then remind yourself of these Scriptures so that you can say the right thing at the right time:

- I have purposed that my mouth shall not transgress. (Ps 17:3)

- Let no corrupt word proceed out of your mouth, but what is good for necessary edification, that it may impart grace to the hearers. (Eph 4:29)

- Fornication and all uncleanness or covetousness, let it not even be named among you, as is fitting for saints; neither filthiness, nor foolish talking, nor coarse jesting, which are not fitting, but rather giving of thanks. (Eph 5:3-4)

In addition to reducing the stress in your life by not speaking negatively, reduce the stress further by speaking positively.

Don't tear yourself down with your own words. Build yourself up speaking positive things from the Word of God about yourself.

Since He Calls those things which do not exist as though they did. (Rom 4:17) And since we have the same spirit of faith, according to what is written, "I believed and therefore I spoke," we also believe and therefore speak. (2 Cor 4:13)

So believe and speak out these Scriptures:

- I can do all things through Christ who strengthens me. (Phil 4:13)

- I am fearfully and wonderfully made (Ps 139:14)

- The Lord will perfect that which concerns me (Ps 138:8)

YOU:

YOUR PAST

Your past is the past because it has passed. Leave it behind where it belongs for what has happened and cannot "unhappen" and trying to make it "unhappen" only brings you unhappiness.

Forgive and forget those who have hurt you. Give them to God for **It is God who avenges** (2 Sam 22:48) and do not tarnish your present and future by revenging.

Copy Joseph who forgave his brothers for selling him into slavery for **Joseph said to them, "Do not be afraid, for am I in the place of God? ... I will provide for you and your little ones." And he comforted them and spoke kindly to them.** (Gen 50:19-21)

Ask God to heal the painful memories and take away the terrifying nightmares. Speak to a Pastor, Christian counselor or trusted adult if the painful experiences mar your relationships.

Then learn from your mistakes and then heed Paul who says, **One thing I do, forgetting those things which are behind and reaching forward to those things which are ahead, I press toward the goal for the prize of the upward call of God in Christ Jesus. Therefore let us, as many as are mature, have this mind** (Phil 3:13-15)

Leave your yesterdays behind and today, begin moving confidently towards your tomorrows believing you have a great future for **I know the thoughts that I think toward you, says the Lord, thoughts of peace and not of evil, to give you a future and a hope.** (Jer 29:11)

YOU:

YOUR FUTURE

To ensure success in your future:

🌲 Take responsibility for your life today.

Your life is a book whose front cover is the day you were born and back cover the day you die. Your parents / guardians wrote the first few chapters for you during your childhood and you begin writing in it for yourself in your teenage years. Each new day is a fresh page for you to compose your life story by the choices you make and their resultant consequences.

So chose your words and actions carefully for **The prudent considers well his steps** (Prov 14:15) and you may not be able to erase their negative effects from your life even though God will forgive you if you ask Him to.

🌲 Visualize where you want to go, what you want to achieve and then **Write the vision and make it plain on tablets, that he may run who reads it.** (Hab 2:2)

E.g. If you want to be a great judge and go to heaven, visualize yourself studying law at the institution of your choice and then sitting in court making judgments that please to God.

After visualizing, plan how you will make your dream a reality. E.g. Research the subjects you need to pass to be accepted into law school.

Then pray and ask God to help you for **A man's heart plans his way, but the Lord directs his steps.** (Prov 16:9)

🌲Pray for God's guidance before you make any move for, **In all your ways acknowledge Him and He shall direct your paths. (Prov 3:6)**

To hear His directions, you have to listen to Him so set aside time to read your Bible and pray everyday. **When you pray, go into your room, and when you have shut your door, pray to your Father who is in the secret place; and your Father who sees in secret will reward you openly.** (Matt 6:6) If you don't have your own room, you can pray silently in class before the 1st lesson or on your bed or on your way to school.

Pray during the good times when all is right and the bad times when you have problems trusting that He will help you. Then do your best, **Commit your way to the Lord, trust also in Him, and He shall bring it to pass. (Ps 37:5)**

🌲Do your best for **Do you see a man who excels in his work? He will stand before kings; he will not stand before unknown men. (Prov 22:29)**

Do your best when doing your class work, home work and other activities like drama, singing, playing musical instruments or games.

In addition, always make the best decisions by asking yourself if the choice you choose will keep you on the path to your vision or if it will derail you.

E.g. if you are offered drugs, ask yourself if using them will keep you on the path to being a heaven bound judge or if it will derail you to the fast track to a mental hospital or jail?

🌲 **Be strong and of good courage** (Josh 1:6) as God told Joshua just before he led the Israelites into the promised land. **Be strong and very courageous, that you may observe to do according to all the law** (Josh 1:7) for it takes guts to go against popular culture and ignore people's disapproval and live as God says.

This Book of the law shall not depart from your mouth, but you shall meditate in it day and night, that you may observe to do according to all that is written in it. For then you will make your way prosperous, and then you will have good success.

Have I not commanded you?

Be strong and of good courage; do not be afraid, nor be dismayed, for the Lord your God is with you wherever you go. (Josh 1:8-9)

🌲 Meditate on (think about) Scriptures like these which reinforce your belief that you will succeed:

🌲 I can do all things through Christ who strengthens me. (Phil 4:13)

- The Lord will perfect that which concerns me (Ps 138:8)

- With God all things are possible (Mark 10:27)

- *In all these things I am more than a conqueror through Him* (ADP Rom 8:37)

- *The Lord is faithful, who will establish me and guard me from the evil one.* (ADP 2 Thess 3:3)

Take your daily Spiritual Vitamins (Rom 12)

Abhor evil **B**less, don't curse **C**ling to good **D**on't conform to the world **E**xude generosity **F**eed enemies **G**ive pals preference **H**umbly relate with peers **I**n hope rejoice **J**ust live in peace **K**indly be friendly **L**ove without hypocrisy **M**uster patience in trials **N**ever revenge **O**vercome evil with good **P**resent your body as a living sacrifice to God **Q**uit being a know-it-all **R**ejoice with the glad **S**erve God **T**hink soberly **U**se your gifts **V**eto defeat by evil **W**eep with the sad e**X**punge reprisals **Y**es, defeat bad with good **Z**ealously pray

ABOUT THE AUTHOR

Dr. Miriam Kinai is a medical doctor who received her Clinical Training in Mind Body Medicine from Harvard Medical School. She is also a trained Christian counselor.

You can visit her blog at
http://www.ChristianStressManagement.com

or follow her on twitter at
http://twitter.com/AlmasiHealth

Email enquiries to drkinai@yahoo.com with BOOKS as your subject.

Other Books by Dr Miriam Kinai

Managing Stress with the Word of God

Managing Stress with the Word of God teaches you effective stress management by combining Biblical principles with medical relaxation techniques.

Topics covered in this book include:

1. What is stress?

2. What is the body's response to stress?

3. Symptoms of Stress

4. 7 Biblical Principles for Stress Management

5. 7 Medical Relaxation Techniques

6. Other Stress Relief Activities

RULES OF RELAXATION

Rules of Relaxation teaches you 130 medical relaxation techniques, mental stress management tactics, spiritual stress relief tips and other multiple other ways to manage stress.

It covers the A to Z of stress management from Assert yourself, Breathe deeply, Cast your burdens, Drink herbal teas, Establish social support, Formulate realistic goals, Guard your heart, Have complementary hobbies, Identify personal stressors, Jaunt, Keep the Sabbath, Listen to music, Meditate on the Word, Nab a nap, Optimize stress, Pamper yourself, Quash sin, Reason rationally, Schedule news fasts, Trust God, Use cognitive restructuring, Veto worry, Work out, eXperiment with aromatherapy, Yield to God to Zap job stress so that you can manage stress more effectively and live through stressful situations without getting distressed.

SWORD WORDS

SWORD WORDS teaches you how to wage your Christian spiritual warfare using the SWORD of the Spirit which is the WORD of God. (Ephesians 6:17)

It instructs you on how to wield your SWORD WORDS together with the full armor of God. It demystifies the enemy's devices and explains the battle plan. It also tells you how to position yourself strategically and communicate effectively with your backup so that you can win your battles regardless of whether you are fighting for your marriage, children, ministry or finances or fighting against addictions, opposition, fear and discouragement.

Made in the USA
San Bernardino, CA
02 February 2013